Cristina Byrne

Romanian for Beginners

Oppian Press
Helsinki, 2020
ISBN 978-951-877-073-5

OPPIAN

Chapter 1   *Romanian basics*

1.   Romanian alphabet and pronunciation

Romanian orthography does not use accents or diacritics – these are secondary symbols added to letters (i.e. basic glyphs) to alter their pronunciation or to distinguish between words. There are, however, five special letters in the Romanian alphabet (associated with four different sounds) which are formed by modifying other Latin letters; strictly speaking these letters function as basic glyphs in their own right rather than letters with diacritical marks, but they are often referred to as the latter.

Vowels

Letter	*Name*	*Phoneme*	*Approximate pronunciation*
A, a	a	/a/	a in "father"
Ă, ă	ă (a with breve)	/ə/	a in "above"
Â, â	î / î din a (a with circumflex)	/ɨ/	
E, e	e	/e/	e in "merry"
I, i	i	/i/	i in "machine"
Î, î	î / î din i		
O, o	o	/o/	o in "floor"
U, u	u	/u/	u in "group"

Consonants

Letter	*Name*	*Phoneme*	*Approximate pronunciation*
B, b	be / bî	/b/	b in "ball"
C, c	ce / cî	/k/	c in "scan"
D, d	de / dî	/d/	d in "door"
F, f	ef / fe / fî	/f/	f in "flag"
G, g	ge / ghe / gî	/g/	g in "goat"
H, h	haș / ha / hî	/h/	h in „hat"
J, j	je / jî	/ʒ/	s in "treasure"
K, k	ca / capa	/k/	c in "scan"
L, l	el / le / lî	/l/	l in "lamp"
M, m	em / me / mî	/m/	m in "morning"
N, n	en / ne / nî	/n/	n in "north"
P, p	pe / pî	/p/	p in "port"
Q, q	chiu	/k/	k in "kettle"
R, r	er / re / rî	/r/	r in „rolling"
S, s	es / se / sî	/s/	s in "song"
Ș, ș	șe / șî	/ʃ/	sh in "shopping"
T, t	te / tî	/t/	t in "stone"
Ț, ț	țe / țî	/ts/	zz in "pizza"
V, v	ve / vî	/v/	v in "vision"
W, w	dublu ve / dublu vî		w in word
X, x	ics	/ks/	x in "six"
Y, y	igrec / i grec	/j/	y in "yes"
Z, z	ze / zet / zed / z	/z/	z in "zipper"

While both „â" and "î „ have the same sound, you will encounter „î" only in the begining of the word like in the word „Încă" and "â„ in

Letters K, Q, W, and Y appear only in foreign borrowings; the pronunciation of W and Y depends on the origin of the word they appear in.

Letter groups

Ce – as „che" in check

Ci – as chi in chimpanzee

Chi – as ke in keen

Che - as ke in keg

Ge – as „ge" in german

Ghe - as „ge" in get

Ghi – as „gi" in give

Diphthongs:

Note: Put the two vowel sounds together to make the diphthong sound.

i (ee) + e (eh) = ie (yeh)

o (oh) + a (ah) = oa (wah)

Example:

Iepure - rabbit

Oameni – humans / people

Nouns –Singular (Substantivul - singular)

The gender of nouns in the singular

Recognizing the gender of Romanian nouns can be difficult for several reasons:

1. Romanian is the only Romance language that preserved three genders from the Latin: masculine, feminine, and neuter. The distinctive part of the neuter gender in Romanian is that it does not have any formal particularities. The neuter nouns in the singular look like masculine nouns, while in the plural they look like feminine nouns. The same applies to adjectives, pronouns and pronominal adjectives. When they modify or replace a neuter noun in the singular they appear in their masculine singular form, and when they modify or substitute a neuter noun in the plural they appear in their feminine plural form.

2. The gender of many inanimate nouns is arbitrary in terms of extralinguistic categories. For instance, the following nouns belonging to

the same thematic group, have different grammatical genders: *pantof –
pantofi* shoe is masculine, *palton – paltoane* winter coat is neuter, and
fustă – fuste skirt is feminine

3. The dictionary form of a noun (i.e. the nominative sing. form)
does not help much in recognizing its gender since there are no formal
markers that can indicate without ambiguity the gender of a noun.
There are several ways of establishing the gender of an independent
noun in Romanian.

1. Noun ending

- all native nouns ending in a **consonant** or -**u** are masculine or neuter;
  however, some borrowed proper names or diminutives in a **consonant**
  or -**u** are feminine: **Carmen, Irinel, Lulu**

- most nouns ending in -**e** are feminine (specific suffixes, such as -**toare,
  -oare, -are, -ere, -ire**, etc. also help to distinguish the feminine from
  the masculine), but a small number are masculine and a few are neuter

- all nouns ending in -**ă**, -**a** ,-**ea**/-**ia** are feminine; however, there are
  some nouns designating male persons that are masculine although
  their ending is -*ă: tată* (father), *popă* (priest), *Papă*(Pope)

- nouns ending in -**i** can be masculine, neuter or feminine

- all feminine nouns end in a vowel (-**ă**, -**a**, -**e**, -**i**)

- there are some borrowed nouns in Romanian with non-typical
  endings, such as -**o**: *radio* (radio), *flamingo* (flamingo). These nouns
  are neuter if they do not designate animate objects. When such a noun
  designates an animate object, its grammatical gender is determined
  by the natural gender of its designate.

2. The 'one-two' test

This method requires the ability to form the plural of the nouns.
Native speakers of Romanian often do this to determine the gender of an
inanimate noun.

The numerals **un** – **o**(one) and **doi** – **două** (two) have masculine
and feminine forms (**un** and **doi** are masculine, while **o** and **două** are
feminine). The neuter nouns act as masculine in the singular and as
feminine in the plural. Accordingly:

- if the masculine numerals **un – doi** go with the singular and the plural of a noun, the noun is masculine: *un bărbat – doi bărbați* (man), *un copil – doi copii* (child), *un pantof – doi pantofi* (shoe), *un copac – doi copaci* (tree)
- if the feminine numerals **o – două** go with the singular and the plural of a noun, the noun is feminine: *o studentă – două student* (student f.), *o plantă – două plante* (plant), *o cafea – două cafele* (coffee), *o zi – două zile* (day)
- if the singular of a noun takes the masculine numeral **un**, and the plural takes the feminine numeral două, the noun is neuter: *un caiet – două caiete* (notebook), *un hotel – două hoteluri* (hotel), *un scaun – două scaune* (chair), *un nume – două nume* (name)

Nouns – Plural (Substantivul – plural)

Masculine nouns are the easiest to decline in Romanian, as there is very little irregularity. All masculine nouns (even those with irregular plurals, such as om (oameni) end in -i. This letter is added to the end of a noun, but in most cases vowel or consonant mutations in the root also occur (like t transforming in ț or s in ș)

Masculine nouns are generally not difficult to identify. The usually end in consonants, -u, -e or -i. Because neuter nouns can also end in all of these, they can sometimes take a bit of work to differentiate, however, masculine and neuter nouns generally end in different consonants.

Masculine nouns ending in consonants will generally end in:

- c (-ic),

  un copac - doi copaci
- l (-il)

  un copil – doi copii
- n (-an, -ean, -ân)

  un fan - doi fani 0
- t (-ist),

  un bărbat – doi bărbați
- r (-or, -tor, -ar, -er)

  un castor – doi castori
- z (-ez)

  un englez – doi englezi

Feminine nouns are relatively complex in the Romanian language.

- -ă changes to -e
  - o studentă - două studente
  - o casă - două case
- -ă changes to -i
  - o maşină - două maşini
  - o seară - două seri
- -ă changes to -uri
  - o marfă - două mărfuri
  - o blană - două blănuri
- -e changes to -i
  - o lume - două lumi
  - o noapte - două nopţi
- -vowel+ie changes to -vowel+i
  - o cheie - două chei
  - o foaie - două foi
- -consonant+ie changes to -consonant+ii
  - o bucătărie - două bucătării
- -ea changes to -ele
  - o stea - două stele
  - o cafea - două cafele
- -i does not change
  - o marţi - două marţi

Articles

As in English, Romanian the articles precede the noun to which they refer.

A. Indefinite Articles

An / A	Un (masculine, singular)
An / A	O (feminine, singular)
Some	Nişte / unele / unii

Examples:

Adrian is a good father.

Adrian este un tată bun

Cristina has a book.

Cristina are o carte

Some kids are outside.

Niște copii sunt afară.

Some of the men are out

Unii bărbați sunt afară

Some of the women are away

Unele femei sunt plecate

B. Definite Articles

Singular

The definite articles come after the noun, added as a suffix .
If the word ends in a consonant, add –ul:

Example

Om – omul
Bărbat – bărbatul
Sat - satul
Oraș - orașul

If the words end in –ă it gets transformed in a

Example

Fată - Fata
Casă – Casa
Rață – Rața
Masă – Masa

If the words end in –u , add –l

Example

Erou – eroul
Sacou – Sacoul
Panou - Panoul
Ou - oul

Plural

For a masculine noun, the definite article is „i" and it is added at the end of the word. The article is preceded by the plural ending.

Oameni - oamenii
Bărbați – Bărbații
Eroi – Eroii

For a feminine or neutre word(having the plural in the feminine form), the definite article „le" is added at the end of the word, after the plural ending.

Sate – Satele
Orașe – Orașele
Fete – Fetele
Case – Casele
Rațe – Rațele
Mese – Mesele
Sacouri – Sacourile
Panouri – Panourile
Ouă – Ouă

Chapter vocabulary

Bărbat – Man	marţi – Tuesday
bărbat –man	Masă – Table
blană - fur	maşină - car
bucătărie - kitchen	noapte - night
cafea - coffee	Om – human
caiet – notebook	Oraş - city
Casă – House	Ou - egg
castor –beaver	palton - coat
cheie - chei	Panou - panel
copac - tree	pantof –shoe
copil –child	popă – priest
englez –Englishman	radio – radio
Erou – Hero	Raţă – duck
fan - fan	Sacou – jacket
Fată - Girl	Sat - village
foaie - sheet of paper	scaun – chair
fustă –skirt	seară - evening
hotel – hotel	stea - star
lume – people / worlds	studentă - student
marfă - merchendise	tată – father

Chapter 2. Greetings and introductions – Saluturi şi introducţie

1. Greetings - Saluturi

Pronouns

The English pronouns (I, you, he, she, we, etc.) are the same in Romanian. The only exception is that Romanian has a singular and plural form for "you".

ROMANIAN - ENGLISH

Eu - I

Tu - You

El - He

Ea - She

Noi - We

Voi - You (plural)

Ei - They (masculine)

Ele - They (feminine)

Notes:

1. If there is a group of masculine and feminine nouns, then it is always referred to by the pronoun **ei**.

2. If a person wishes to address someone (or group of people) in a formal tone, the speaker would use the pronoun **DUMNEAVOASTRĂ**. The verb's form for this pronoun is the same as for **voi**.

Example

Dumneavoastră sunteţi din România?

You (respectfully) are from Romania?

Domnişoară - Miss

Doamnă – Madam / lady

Domn - Mister

Common short questions

Who – Cine
When – Când
Where – Unde
What – Ce
How – Cum
Why – De ce
For what – Pentru ce

2. *Pronoun cases*

Personal pronouns have two sets of forms in the accusative. There is a series of stressed (full) forms, and a series of unstressed (clitic) forms

Nominativ	Accusative	
	Stressed(Full)	Unstressed(Clitic)
Eu	(pe) mine	Mă (-mă, mă-, m-)
Tu	(pe) tine	Te (-te, te-)
El	(pe) el	Îl (-l, l-)
Ea	(pe) ea	O (-o, o-)
Noi	(pe) noi	Ne (-ne, ne-)
Voi	(pe) voi	Vă (-vă, vă-, v-)
Ei	(pe) ei	Îi (-I, I-)
Ele	(pe) ele	Le (-le, le-)

The stressed forms of the personal pronouns in the accusative are always preceded by a preposition, such as: **pe** (on), **la** (at), **cu** (with), **pe la** (at), **pentru** (for), **lângă** (next to), **fără** (without), **ca** (as, like, than) etc. The preposition **pe** is used both as a morphological marker without lexical meaning (indicating the direct object), and as a preposition with the lexical meaning 'on'

Te vreau <u>pe tine</u>- I want you (pe without lexical meaning)

Am fost <u>la tine</u>- I was at your place

Am fost <u>cu tine</u>- I was with you

Am ceva <u>pentru tine</u> – I have something for you

Unstressed forms

Vă aştept – I wait for you

O aştept - I wait for her

Ei ne aşteaptă – They are waiting for us (You can also find it as ne-aşteaptă)

The personal pronoun used as a direct object

When the personal pronoun is a direct object and a substitute for nouns that do not designate human beings, the unstressed forms of the 3rd person are used:

Punem <u>cartea</u> aici. **We put the book here.**
We put the book here

<u>Îl</u> punem aici. **We put it here.**
We place it here

Punem <u>cana</u> pe masă. **We put the cup here.**
We put the cup on the table

<u>O</u> punem pe masă. **We put it here.**
We put it on the table

Am auzit <u>un zgomot</u>. **We heard a noise.**
I heard a noise

<u>L</u>-am auzit. **We heard it.**
I heard it

Vom citi <u>o poveste</u>. **We'll read a story.**
We will read a story

<u>O</u> vom citi. **We'll read it.**
We will read it

When being a direct object and a substitute for nouns that designate human beings, the unstressed forms of the personal pronoun in all persons can be used, alone or accompanied by the equivalent full form :

<u>Mă</u> aştepţi? (<u>Mă</u> aştepţi <u>pe mine</u>?)
Will you wait for me ?

<u>Te</u> ascult. (Te ascult <u>pe tine</u>.)
I'm listening to you.

<u>Îl / o</u> iubesc. (<u>Îl</u> iubesc <u>pe el</u>. / <u>O</u> iubesc <u>pe ea</u>.)
I love him / her.

<u>Ne</u> aşteptaţi? (<u>Ne</u> aşteptaţi <u>pe noi</u>?)
Will you wait for us ?

<u>Vă</u> aşteptăm. (<u>Vă</u> aşteptăm <u>pe voi</u>.)
We will wait for you.

<u>Îi / le</u> aşteptăm. (<u>Îi</u> aşteptăm <u>pe ei</u>. Le aşteptăm <u>pe ele</u>.)
We are waiting for them (masc. / fem.)

For interrogations, Romanian is different than English. For example "Are you coming?" will be translated as "Tu vii?". If it was translated as "Vii tu?" itwould express a feeling of wonder.

The stressed forms are used either independently, in isolated constructions, or for emphasis. When used as direct objects designating human beings, the stressed forms of the personal pronoun in the accusative are preceded by the preposition **pe** (the preposition **pe** in this structure does not have lexical meaning, but only the function of a grammatical marker of the accusative case of people), and are used together with the corresponding unstressed forms:

- <u>**Te iubesc pe tine**</u>. I love you (I don't love someone else).

- **Pe mine?** (Do you love) me ?

- **Da, <u>pe tine</u>!** Yes, (I love) you !

In other words, in such structures the unstressed forms of the personal pronoun are required, while the presence of the stressed forms is optional.

Full and clitic forms of the dative

Like for the accusative, the personal pronoun has two sets of forms in the dative : stressed (full) forms and unstressed (clitic) forms.

Nominativ	Dative	
	Stressed(Full)	Unstressed(Clitic)
Eu	Mie	Îmi (-mi, mi-)
Tu	Ţie	Îţi (-ţi. ţi-)
El	Lui	Îi (-I, I-)
Ea	Ei	
Noi	Nouă	Ne (-ne, ne-)
Voi	Vouă	Vă (-vă, v- , vi)
Ei	Lor	Le(-le, le-, li)
Ele		

– in the 3rd person singular there are two stressed dative forms, one for masculine (**lui**) and one for feminine (**ei**); the unstressed forms are identical (**îi, -i-**)

– in the 3rd person plural there is no gender opposition

The unstressed forms of the personal pronouns in the dative, like those in the accusative, always accompany a verb:

Îmi aduce Ion geanta. Ion is bringing me the bag.

Mi-ai adus geanta? Have you brought me the bag?

Îmi va aduce Ion geanta. Ion will bring me the bag.

The forms beginning with î- (**îmi, îţi, îi**) occur as separate words:

Îmi explici despre ce este vorba? — Can you explain to me what all this is about?

The short equivalent forms without î- (with the î- elided) are always attached to another word that begins or ends in a vowel:

Mi-a explicat despre ce este vorba. He explained to me what all this was about.

The forms ni (1st pers. pl.), vi (2nd pers. pl.) and li (3rd pers. pl.) are used in certain combinations with other unstressed personal pronouns in the

The personal pronoun used as an indirect object

Generally, in order to express the indirect object, the unstressed forms of the personal pronoun in the dative are used: 58

- **Îmi spui adevărul?** Are you telling me the truth ?
- **Îți dau o carte bună.** I'm giving you a good book.

The stressed forms of the personal pronouns in the dative are used independently, in isolated constructions, or as a repetitive element, for emphasis:

- **Îmi aduce Dan cartea.** Dan is bringing me the book.
- **Ție?** To you? **Îmi aduce cartea mie, nu ție!** He's bringing the book to me, not to you !

When the stressed forms of the personal pronouns in the dative are used, the double expression of the indirect object (i.e. using the correlative unstressed form in the same sentence) is required:

- **Vă explic vouă despre ce este vorba, ei știu deja.**
- I'm explaininig to you what all this is about, they already know.
- **Le-ai spus și lor unde mergem mâine?**
- Have you also told them where we are going tomorrow?

As for the direct object, in structures with the indirect object the unstressed forms of the personal pronoun are required, while the presence of the stressed forms is optional.

3. *Possessive Pronouns*

The possessive pronouns/adjectives agree in gender and number with the 'possessed object' and in number with the 'possessor'. Depending on the gender and number of the possessed object, four main forms (masc. and fem. sg. and pl.) are available for each of the three persons:

Singular

Meu - My (masc.)

Câinele meu

Ta - Your (fem.)

Pisica ta

Mea – My (fem.)

Pisica mea

Său / Lui – His (masc.)

Câinele lui

Tău – Your (masc.)

Câinele tău

Sa / Ei - Hers (fem.)

Câinele ei

Plural

Mei – My (masc.)

Câinii mei

Tale – Your (fem.)

Pisicile tale

Mele – My (fem.)

Pisicile mele

Săi / Lui – His (masc)

Câinii lui

Tăi – Your (masc.)

Câinii tăi

Sale / Ei – Her (fem.)

Pisicile ei.

Usual greetings

Bună / Salut (usually used between males)
Hello

Bună dimineața
Good morning

Bună ziua
Good day

Bună seara
Good evening

Noapte bună
Good night

Ce faci? (it litterly means what are you doing?)
How are you?

Bine, mulţumesc.
Fine, thank you.

Îmi pare bine să te cunosc.
Nice to meet you.

Vă rog.
Please.

Mă scuzaţi.
Excuse me.

Scuze.
Sorry.

La revedere.
Goodbye.

Cu plăcere. (literally- with pleasure)
You are welcome.

Noroc!
Cheers!

4. *How to introduce yourself - Cum să te prezinţi*

Gramar corner - To be/ a fi - Present

Present simple		Prezentul simplu	
Afirmative	**Afirmativ**	**Negative**	**Negativ**
I am	Eu sunt	I am not	Eu nu sunt
You are	Tu eşti	You are not	Tu nu eşti
He/she/it is	El /ea este	He / She is not	El/ ea nu este
We are	Noi suntem	We are not	Noi nu suntem
You are	Voi sunteţi	You are not	Voi nu sunteţi
They are	Ei / Ele sunt	They are not	Ei / Ele nu sunt

The conjugation **este** can be shortened to **e**, and it is done quite often in spoken Romanian. It has the same meaning.

The negation of a verb is done by preceding it with **nu**

The last names(nume de familie) in Romanian come before the given name(nume).

Numele meu este Smith John.
My name is John Smith.

Care este numele tău de familie?
What is your last name?

Numele meu este Georgescu .
My name is Georgescu.

Eu sunt George
I am George

Eu sunt din Anglia
I am from England

Eu nu sunt din Anglia
I am not from England

Eu stau în Londra
I live in London

De unde ești?
Where are you from?

Cum te simți?
How are you feeling?

Îți place România?
Do you like Romania?

5. *Adjective - Adjective*

Adjectives in Romanian are much different from adjectives in English. Adjectives agree with nouns in gender, number and case. Unlike in English, the typical place for an adjective in a sentence is **after the noun**, not in front of it. Whenever an adjective preceeds a noun, the intention is purely emphatic.

Most adjectives in Romanian are variable, meaning that they have different forms for masculine, feminine, singular and plural. Adjectives with four forms are the most numerous.

1. *Those that have consonant endings*

El este bun
He is good

+ă for feminine singular
Ea este bună
She is good

+i for masculine plural
Ei sunt buni
They are good

+e for feminine plural
Ele sunt bune
They are good

2. *Those that change their form to agree with the gender of the person or object they describe*

Singular
El este frumos
He is beautiful

Ea este frumoasă
She is beautiful

Plural
Ei sunt frumoşi
They are beautiful

Ele sunt frumoase
They are beautiful (feminine)

3. Those ending with –e in singular form

Paharul este rece
The glass is cold

Paharele sunt reci
The glasses are cold

fierbinte
fierbinți hot, heated

iute
iuți hot, spicy

4. Those ending with – u in singular form

El este mândru
He is proud

-u transforms in – ă for feminine singular
Ea este mândră
She is proud

-u transforms in –i for masculine plural
Ei sunt mândri
They are proud

-u transforms in –e for feminine plural
Ele sunt mândre
They are proud

You will find also that, with the feminine gender, there are several different types of ending for specifying the nationality and that the nationality , as opposed to English , in Romanian is not written with a capital letter.

Example:

Sunt franțuzoaică .
I am French.

But

Sunt suedeză.
I'm Swedish.

Eu sunt româncă.
I am Romanian.

Degrees of Comparison

Positive

inteligent - intelligent

Comparative

mai inteligent decât / ca - more intelligent than
mai puțin inteligent decât / ca - less intelligent than
la fel de inteligent ca - as intellient as

Superlative

cel mai inteligent (relative) the most intelligent
foarte / extraordinar de inteligent (absolute) very intelligent

Expressions that Romanians use

Still in the adjective category are several expressions that function as adjectives and never change their form. Most of the time these expressions refer to human qualities:

de încredere = trustworthy
de treabă = good person to hang with/helpful
fără scrupule = unscrupulous
fără minte = crazy
fără obraz = shameless
cu capul pe umeri = level-headed
cu capul plecat = humble
cu nasul pe sus = full of himself/herself; vain
gust fin = tasteful (lit. smooth taste)

Gramar corner – To be/ A fi – Past tense

Past tense	Trecut
I was	Eu am fost
You were	Tu ai fost
He/She/it was	El/Ea a fost
We were	Noi am fost
You were	Tu ai fost
They were	Ei / Ele au fost

I was from London.
Eu am fost din Londra.

They were here before.
Ei / Ele au fost aici înainte.

We were friends for a long time.
Noi am fost prieteni pentru mult timp.

He was a student.
El a fost student.

Gramar corner – To have/ A avea- Present

Present	**Prezent**
I have	Eu am
You have	Tu ai
He/she/it has	El/ea are
We have	Noi avem
You have	Voi aveți
They have	Ei / Ele au

I have a dog.
Eu am un câine.

I do not have a dog.
Eu nu am un câine.

You have a cat.
Tu ai o pisică.

They have chiken.
Ei / Ele au găini.

I do not have money.
Eu nu am bani.

Hello, I am Ema. I am from Scotland and I came here for a vacantion. I like nature and parks. **Where** do you recomend visiting?

Bună. Sunt Ema. Sunt din Scoția și am venit aici în vacanță. Îmi plac natura și parcurile. **Unde** recomanzi să vizitez?

Gramar corner – To have / A avea – Past tense

Past tense	Trecut
I had	Eu am avut
You had	Tu ai avut
He/ She/it had	El/Ea a avut
We had	Noi am avut
You had	Tu ai avut
They had	Ei / Ele au avut

Practice 1

I. **Choose the right word**

1. Eu ... Andrei.

a) este　　　　　b) sunt　　　　　c) am fost

2. ... faci?

a) Cum　　　　　b) Unde　　　　　c) Ce

3. El ... prietenul meu.

a) sunt　　　　　b) are　　　　　c) este

4. ... avem timp.

a) Noi　　　　　b) Voi　　　　　c) Ei

5. ... ziua

a) Noapte　　　　　b) Bună　　　　　c) Scuze

6. Câinele .... este frumos

a) meu　　　　　b) el　　　　　c) rău

7. ...dai cartea te rog?

a) Eu　　　　　b) Îmi　　　　　c) El

8. Ţi-l dau .... dacă vrei.

a) mie　　　　　b) cartea　　　　　c) ţie

9. Ei.... multe animale.

a) Are　　　　　b) au　　　　　c) sunt

10. Andrei este cel mai...... copil

a) fericit　　　　　b) ferictă　　　　　c) are

II. Translate the following text.

– Good morning.
– I am Andrei and he is Peter. Nice to meet you.
– We are from England. It is colder than Romania. Do you like England?

____

____

– Scuzați-mă. Noi vizităm România.
– Ne puteți spune unde este parcul mare? Vrem să vedem lacul.
– Îți mulțumesc.

____

____

III. Fill in the blanks.

– 1. Ea este ___________(more beautiful)

– 2. Eu sunt __________(Romanian)

– 3. Andrei este _______________________ ca Ion
       (more intelligent)

– 4. Ea _________a dog (has)

– 5. Matei și Ioana _________ o pisică mică (have)

– 6. Ei sunt _________ prieteni (good)

– 7. Noi suntem ___________ de el (proud)

– 8. Ei sunt copii __________(mine)

– 9. ___simți bine? (You)

– 10. Acest cadou este _________________(for you).

Chapter vocabulary

Dimineaţă – morning

Seară – evenening

Noapte – night

Bună – good

Parc – park

Inteligent – intelligent

Deştept – smart

Mândru – proud

Vizită – visit

Rece – cold

Vacanţă – vacantion

Natură – nature

Recomandare – recomendation

Câine –dog

Pisică – cat

Găină – chicken

încredere - trust

treabă - work

fără - without

obraz - cheek

cap - head

umăr – shoulder

plecat – lowered / left / away

nas - nose

sus - up

gust - taste

fin – smooth

scuze –sorry

here – aici

there – acolo

bani - money

înainte –before

cadou- gift

fierbinte - hot

iute –spicy

adevăr –truth

geantă – bag

zgomot - noise

cană – cup

carte – book

poveste – story

masă - table

Chapter 3   At the restaurant – La restaurant

1.   Ordering food – Comandarea mâncării

Depending on the area, most restaurants have an english menu .

Homemade dishes are a world apart, so if invited to have lunch or dinner with a Romanian family, do not miss the opportunity.

As in most countries, independent restaurants tend to be better than hotel restaurants so do not hesitate to visit smaller, privately owned restaurants.

In some regions of Romania, and especially in Transylvania, some dishes may be prepared with more fat than you might usually use.

Instead of having a heavy (meat) dish for lunch, try some delicious Romanian cheese and vegetables, especially during the warm summers.

Salads are usually a side order, which comes with most entrees, especially steaks.

Wine mixed with mineral water ("șpriț") is very popular during summer.

Hot wine with sugar and cinnamon ("vin fiert") is "the recommended drink" for cold winter days.

For something stronger try plum brandy ("țuică") or hot plum brandy with sugar and peppercorn("țuică fiartă").

Gramar corner - To want /A vrea- Present

Present	**Prezent**
I want	Eu vreau
You want	Tu vrei
He / she / it wants	El / ea vrea
We want	Noi vrem
You want	Voi vreți
They want	Ei / Ele vor

I want still water
Eu vreau apă plată

I want a coke
Eu vreau o cola

They want a menu
Ei vor un meniu

Formal speaking.

As in english, romanian has formal speaking as well. When ordering the meal you would use „I **would** like" (Eu **aş** dori) .In many cases the personal pronoun is omitted when speaking. For example:

I would like to start with chicken soup.
(Eu) Aş dori să încep cu supa de pui.

Meal courses

Aperitiv - appetizer
Antreuri - entrées
Desert –dessert
Felul întâi – Main course

You can have the meal „ to go" as in „la pachet"(packed) or you can dine in and it would be „aici" here.

Mâncaţi aici sau la pachet?
Are you eating here or do you want it to go?

Ways of preparing the food:

Prăjit – fried
Copt – baked
La grătar - grilled
La aburi – steamed
Sote - saute
Bine făcut – well done
În sânge – medium rare
Murat – pickled
Afumat – smoked
Marinat – marinated
Decorticat – peeled
Glazurat - glazed
Produs congelat – frozen product

Dinning ustensills:

Furculiță – fork
Lingură – spoon
Lingurița – small spoon
Cuțit – knife
Farfurie – plate
Pahar – glass
Sticlă – bottle
șervețel – napkin
bol – boul

2.   *Payment – Plata*

Romania's currency is Leu (plural "Lei" - pronunciation: *lay*).
Common Abbreviation: RON

Banknote denominations: 1, 5, 10, 50, 100 and 500 lei
Coins: 1, 5, 10 and 50 bani pieces. (pronunciation: *bahnee*)
1 leu = 100 bani

Foreign currencies may be exchanged at banks or authorized exchange offices (called: *"casa de schimb"* or *"birou de schimb valutar"*).
International airports and larger hotels also offer currency exchange services.

Asking for the check:

Nota vă rog .

You have the option to pay eighter with cash or card. Usually the waiter would ask. Tips (bacșiș) is not a requirment in Romania but it is usually expected.

Plătiți cu cash sau card?
Paying with cash or card?

Drinks – Băuturi

Sparkling water – Apă minerală
Still water – Apă plată
Tea - ceai
Juice – Suc
Soda drinks – Băuturi carbogazoase
Coke - Cola

Lemonade – Limonadă
Coffee – Cafea
Hot Chocolate – Ciocolată Caldă
Wine – Vin
Mulled wine – Vin fiert

To ask for more you would use „încă un / o"

Încă o bere vă rog
One more beer please.

3.   *Adverbs of time*

Adverbs of time tell us **when** an action happened, but also **for how long**, and **how often.**

1. *Adverbs that tell us when are usually placed at the end of the sentence.*

Am văzut filmul **ieri.**
I saw the movie **yesterday.**

Voi mâncă supă **mâine.**
I will eat soup **tomorrow.**

Am vazut-o pe Ioana **azi**
I saw Ioana **today.**

Te voi suna mai **târziu**
I will call you **later.**

Trebuie să plec **acum.**
I have to leave **now.**

Am plecat **anul trecut.**
I left **last year.**

Yet is used in questions and in negative sentences to indicate that something that has not happened or may not have happened but is expected to happen. It is placed at the end of the sentence or after not.

N-ai terminat treaba **încă?**
Have you not finished your work **yet?**

Ni, nu **încă.**
No, not **yet.**

Ei nu l-au întâlnit **încă.**
They haven't met him **yet.**

Other adverbs of time

mâine - tomorrow
atunci - then
în seara aceasta - tonight
chiar acum - right now
aseară - last night
în această dimineaţă this morning
săptămâna viitoare - next week
deja - already
de curând - recently
în ultimul timp - lately
în curând - soon
imediat - immediately
în continuare - still
în urmă - ago

2. Adverbs that tell us for how long

Ea a dormit **toată ziua**
She slept **all day**.

Sora mea a trăit în Franţa **pentru un an**
My sister lived in France **for a year**.

3. Adverbs that tell us how often

Adverbs that tell us how often express the frequency of an action.

Dese ori mănânc mâncare vegetariană.
I often eat vegetarian food.

El nu bea lapte **niciodată**.
He **never** drinks milk.

Mereu trebuie să îţi termini mâncarea.
You must **always** finish your food.

El mănâncă **rar** peşte
He **rarely** eats fish.

Other examples

frecvent - frequently
de obicei - usually
uneori - sometimes
ocazional - occasionally

4. și – also / too – adverb

"Și" is very used in the Romanian language and position in a sentence is often different to their equivalents in English and therefore it is important to study these examples

Și eu aș lua tot un ceai
I too would also like a tea

Avem și înghețată și prăjituri
We have both ice cream and cakes

Și pentru mine tot o înghețată
And an ice cream for me too

Altceva mai doriți?
Do you want anything else?

Și Ioana și Matei sunt la restaurant
Both Ioana and Matei are at the restaurant

Mai vrei o cafea?
Do you want another cup of coffee?

George este tot la magazin
George is still at the store

Ana tot vorbește
Ana talks continuously/is still talking

Nicu stă la București (Și Andrei stă tot acolo)
Nicu lives in Bucharest (Andrew lives there too)

4. *Allergies or dietary needs – Alergii sau diete speciale*

In some restaurants or cafes the menu contains a list of the ingredients used in the dishes and it is specified if it contains any alergens but do make sure to check with the waiter.

Possible allergens – Posibili alergeni
Egg – ou
Gluten – gluten
Garlic – Usturoi
Milk- Lapte
Soy – Soia
Peanut – alune
Pepper – Ardei

Oats – Ovăz
Rice – Orez
Sesame – Susan
Wheat – Grâu
GMO – GMO

Eu sunt alergic la alune.
I am allergic to peanuts.

Aveți și fără ou?
Do you have it without egg too?

Am diabet, îndulcitor aveți?
I have diabeetus, do you have sweetner ?

Andreea are alergie la gluten.
Andreea has gluten allergy.

Aș dori fără ardei.
I would like it without peppers.

Doriți ceva de băut?
Would you like something to drink?

Aș dori Cola fără zahăr.
I would like Coke without sugar.

Ea are intoleranță la lactoză
She has lactoze intolerance.

Eu sunt vegetarian.
I am vegetarian.

Ingredients you may want more or less of – Ingrediente din care ai vrea mai mult sau mai puțin

Sugar- Zahăr
Salt – Sare
Pepper –Piper
Onion – Ceapă
Tomato – Roșie
Mayo – Maioneză
Ketchup – Ketchup
Mustard – Muștar
Olive oil – Ulei de măsline

Vinegar – Oțet
Cheese – Brânză
Sweetener – Îndulcitor
Honey – Miere

Ordering food example

Bună ziua, as dori o apă plată și un pahar de vin alb.

Vreau o friptură de vită la grătar , bine făcută,cu legume la aburi dar fără ardei și ceapă. În plus vreau o salată de vară cu extra roșii. Sos de maioneză și barbecue lângă. Nu vreau desert. Mulțumesc.

Se poate plăti cu cardul?

Good day, I would like a still water and a glass of white wine.

I want a well done grilled steak with steamed vegetables but without peppers and onion. Also i would like a summer salad with extra tomatoes. Mayo and ketchup too. I donât want dessert. Thank you.

Can i pay with the card?

Practice 2

I. **Fill in the blanks.**

– 1. Eu _________ o cola. (want)

– 2. El _________ vegetarian. (is)

– 3. El vrea o salată________ brânză.(without)

– 4. Noi am dori o pizza___________________________________
(with more mushrooms)

– 5. Nu doresc _______________________(fries).

– 6. Un burger ________________ vă rog. (without mayo)

– 7. _______ de pui aveți? (Soup)

– 8. Pastele ____________________? (have milk)

– 9. Tocănița este ___________?(spicy)

– 10. Aveți _______________ cu semințe?(bread)

II. Translate the following to English

- 1. Bună seara. Aş dori un pahar de vin roşu şi o cafea.

- 2. Nu doresc cartofi prăjiţi. Îi vreau copţi.

- 3. Sunt alergic la ou, se poate înlocui?

- 4. Aş dori un pahar de ţuică.

- 5. Meniu vegetarian aveţi?

- 6. O îngheţată de căpşuni vă rog.

- 7. Tocăniţa de ceapă este picantă?

- 8. Îmi puteţi aduce un pliculeţ de zahăr brun?

- 9. Îndulcitor sau miere aveţi?

- 10. O porţie de sarmale cu smântână.

III. Translate the following to Romanian

- 1. Hello, I would like a jasmine tea with honey.
- 2. Could I have the drink menu?
- 3. I would like a medium rare steak.
- 4. Can I have one more lemonade?
- 5. How big is the portion?
- 6. Can i have the check please?
- 7. Do you serve shrimp?
- 8. Does this contain gluten?
- 9. Could she have another fork?
- 10. Do you have a children menu?

Chapter vocabulary

alb – white

Alergie – allergy

Altceva – something alse

Apă mineral – sparkling water

Apă plată – still water

Bani – money

Băutură- drink

Bere – beer

cartofi prăjiți - fries

Căpșuni - strawberries

Ceva – something

Ciorbă – broth

Creveți - shrimp

Diabet –diabetus

Fără - without

Film - movie

Foame – hunger

Friptură – steak

iasomie – jasmine

Intoleranță – intolerant

Încep – start

Înghețată –ice cream

Lactoză – lactose

Magazine – store

Mâncare – food

meniu –menu

Mult- much

Nevoie – need

Notă de plată – check

paste – pasta

pâine - bread

pește - fish

picant - spicy

Plată – payment

Prăjitură – cake

Pui – chicken

Puțin – little / less

Restaurant- restaurant

roșu –red

Sarmale- cabbage rolls

semințe - seeds

Smântână – sour cream

Suna –give a call

Supă – soup

șpriț - wine mixed
with sparkling water

tocăniță - stew

țuică – plum brandy

Vegetarian – vegetarian

Vorbește – talks

Chapter 4   At a hotel - La hotel

1.   Booking a room- Rezervarea camerii

When booking a room you have to think about the accomodations you
wish to have . For example room are:

Nefumători – non – smoking
Fumători – smoking
De o persoană - one person room
Dublă – double
Triplă – triple
Cu baie privată – with private bathroom
Baie pe hol – shared bathroom (on hallway)
Cu cadă – with bathtub
Cu duş - with shower
Izolată fonic – sound proof
Cu bucătărie – with kitchen
Cu vedere panoramică – with panoramic view
Mic dejun inclus – breakfast included
Totul inclus – all inclusive

The week in Romania starts with Monday and not Sunday. Also, the days
are not written with a capital letter when it is not at the begining of the
sentence.

Days	*Zile*
Week	Săptămână
Monday	Luni
Tuesday	Marţi
Wednesday	Miercuri
Thursday	Joi
Friday	Vineri
Saturday	Sâmbătă
Sunday	Duminică

Today	***Astăzi***
Yesterday	Ieri
Tomorrow	Mâine
This week	Săptămâna aceasta
Last week	Săptămâna trecută
Next week	Săptămâna viitoare

Months	***Lunile anului***
January	Ianuarie
February	Februarie
March	Martie
April	Aprilie
May	Mai
June	Iunie
July	Iulie
August-	August
September	Septembrie
October	Octombrie
November	Noiembrie
December	Decembrie

Aş dori să fac o rezervare pentru săptămâna viitoare.
I would like to make a booking for next week.

Aveţi o cameră care permite animale de companie?
Do you a room that allows pets?

Aş dori o cameră de ne-fumători.
I would like a non-smoking room.

Aveţi o cameră dublă cu baie?
Do you have a double room with bathroom?

Example:

Bună ziua, aş dori să rezerv o cameră pentru miercuri, săptămâna următoare. Vreau o cameră dublă, baie cu cadă dacă se poate, să permită animale mici, am o pisică, şi de nefumători. Se poate şi cu mic dejun inclus?

Good day, I would like to book a room for wednesday, next week. I want a double room, with a tub in the bathroom if possible, that allows pets, I have a cat, and for non–smokers. Is it possible with breakfast included?

2. *Checking in / out*

In Romanian the terms „check in" and „check out" are used frequently even by non English speakers but it usually comes with „-ul". This happens to English words that are borrowed in the language: „**router**ul", „**T.V.**-ul"(red as: te ve-ul), „**skateboard**ul", „**p.c.**-ul", „**weekend**ul", „**mouse**ul", „**whiskey**-ul" etc.

Bună ziua, am o rezervare făcută săptămâna trecută pe numele Bradu Alin pentru o cameră dublă de nefumători.

Good day, i have a booking made last week with the name Bradu Alin for a non–smoking double room.

Mă scuzați, se poate să fac check in-ul mai devreme?
Excuse me, is it possible to do the check in earlier?

Aceasta este cartea mea de identitate.
This is my identity card.

Când trebuie eliberată camera?
When do i have to check out?

Vă predau cheia la plecare?
Do i give you the key when i leave?

Pot verifica informația?
Can I check the info?

3. *Common problems – Probleme comune*

Romania's electrical current is 230 V -- 50 cycles; sockets take the standard continental European dual round-pronged plugs.

A plug adaptor may be required for non-European appliances. A power converter is necessary for appliances requiring 110 V

While the hotel clerk may speak english the other employees may not. Here are some problems or questions that could come up.

Romanians use "merge" as well as "funcționează" to express the word "works" for utilities, electonics or software.

Nu merge internetul.
The internet is not working.

Nu este curent.
The electricity is out.

Nu funcționează aerul coniționat.
The air conditioner is not working.

Televizorul nu funcționează.
The T.V is not working.

Întrerupătorul este blocat.
The switch is stuck.

Nu merge priza.
The wall socket is not working.

Am nevoie de un prosop.
I need a towel

Nu este hârtie igienică la baie.
There is no toilet paper in the bathroom.

Scurgerea este înfundată.
The drain is clogged.

Când este prânzul?
When is the lunch?

Unde se servește cina?
Where is the dinner served?

Aveți o pătură în plus?
Do you have an extra blanket?

Unde este spălătoria?
Where is the laundry room?

Puteți schimba lenjeria de pat?
Can you change the bed sheets?

Vecinii sunt prea gălăgioși.
The neighbours are too loud.

Geamul este blocat.
The window is stuck.

Nu merge cheia.
The key doesn't work.

Am uitat bagajul.
I forgot the luggage.

Nu găsesc cheia.
I can't fiind the key.

Am pierdut cheia.
I lost the key.

Nu merge apa caldă.
The hot water isn't running.

Practice 3

I. Fill in the blanks.

– 1. Aş dori o cameră_____________________(single)

– 2. Aş dori o _________ suplimentară (blanket)

– 3. Permiteţi să vin cu un _____________?(pet)

– 4. La ce oră este _____________?(breakfast)

– 5. Camera disponibilă este _____________________?
(sound proof)

– 6. Care _______este parola la internet?(is)

– 7. _______________este spart. (the window)

– 8. În ce _______ sosiţi? (month)

– 9. Vom elibera camera ___________(Saturday)

– 10. Am sunat ___________ (last week)

– 11. Când este _____________ camera triplă?(available)

– 12. Pot avea un alt ___________?(towel)

– 13. Vreau să verific _________. (the booking)

– 14. Aceasta este _________ dumneavoastră.(key)

– 15. Când este servită ___________?(dinner)

II. Translate the phrases into English.

1. Bună seara, aş dori să rezerv o cameră triplă pentru miercuri.
   Am văzut că sunt permise animalele de companie, este adevărat?
2. Camera disponibilă este pentru nefumători?
3. Avem o problemă şi ajungem mai târziu,
   putem face check in-ul atunci?
4. Putem lua micul dejun dacă plătim?
5. Aveţi cameră disponibilă pentru luna viitoare?
6. Pot fuma în cameră?
7. Bucătăria este comună?
8. Unde este baia comună?
9. Spălătoria este deschisă mereu?
10. Îmi puteţi da încă un set de prosoape vă rog?

III. Translate the phrases into Romanian.

1. Hello, could I book a double room
   with shared bathroom for Tuesday of this week?

2. Is it possible to have a later check out?

3. Is the room on the top floor sound proofed?

4. The hot water is not running in the room.

5. Can the clogged drain be fixed today?

6. Until when is breakfast served?

7. Do I have access to the shared kitchen all day?

8. The internet is not working in my room.

9. The bathroom has a bathtub or a shower?

10. When is the check out?

Chapter vocabulary

a fuma – to smoke

a permite- to allow

a servi – to serve

a suna – to call

a verifica- to verify

acces – access

adevărat – true

alt –another

bagaj -luggage

Camera- room

cheie – key

comună – shared

deshis – open / light

disponibil – available

double – dublă

Hotel – hotel

inclus – included

informație – information

izolată- izolated

în plus – to add/ more

înfundată – clogged

oră – hour

parolă – password

problemă – problem

prosop –towel

set – set

spart – broken

spălatorie – laundry room

Suplimentară – extra

târziu – late

triplă – triple

a găsi – to find

Chapter 5   Shopping - Cumpărături

While Romania has supermarkets and stores you will fiind yourself among many traditional farmer'a market with varried products from vegetables and fruits to meat and milk product. From spring to fall you can find many fresh products for a very small price.

This markets sometimes invite the customer to taste their product to make it easier to decide on which to buy. In the market, the only way to pay is with cash.

Romania uses the metric system so you will mostly deal with kilograms(kilograme) and litres (litri).

The sellers are usually the farmers themselves or employed people that rarely speak english. You can easily buy as so:

Aş dori un kilogram de pere.
I would like a kg of pears.

Cât face?
How much is it?

Cât este kilogramul?
How much is the kg? (value)

Puneţi de 5 lei.
Put up to 5 lei.

Un kilogram de roşii şi de restul cartofi.
A kilogram of tomatoes and for the rest
(of the money given) potatoes.

Mâncarea este mai ieftină la supermarket
decât la magazinul de la colţ.
The food is cheaper at the market than at the corner store.

Imperial system to Metric :

1 mile equals 1.6 Kilometers.

1 inch is about 25 millimeters or 2.54 centimeters

1 litre is 1000 mililitres (mililitri)

A 3-foot measurement is almost exactly 1 meter

1 Kilogram is just over 2 pounds

1 pound is about 454 grams

For British visitors, 100 pounds = 7.14 stone

Practice 4

I. Translate the following phrases in English

1. Dați-mi un kilogram de cartofi și două de ceapă.

2. Asta este tot ce aveți?

3. Cât este un litru de lapte?

4. Îmi puteți pune bucata aceea?

5. Vreau 500 de grame de măsline.

6. Aveți să îmi dați rest?

7. Unde etse piața?

8. De restul puneți mere.

9. Pot alege eu?

10. Dumneavoastră creșteți legumele?

____

____

____

____

____

____

____

____

____

____

____

____

____

II. Translate the phrases in Romanian

1. How much is a kilogram of tomatoes?

2. I would like to buy a bag of cookies.

3. Do you have a different size?

4. Do you accept cash?

5. May I have two of the same?

6. A kg of potatoes and a kilogram of onions please.

7. Do you have it in 2 litre bottles?

8. Two 330 mililitres beers please.

9. How much is the 330 militres compared to the 500 mililitres one?

10. Is a piece cheaper than the package?

Chapter vocabulary

a alege – to choose

a compara – to compare

a creşte – to grow

bucată - piece

colţ - corner

comparativ –compared

kilogram –kilogram

kilometru – kilometre

litru- litre

livră (weight)/ liră
(for money) - pound

magazin – shop

mărime – size

milă – mile

numerar – cash

pachet – package

piaţă - farmerţs market

pungă – bag

rest – left over

sticlă – bottle

supermarket – supermarket

Chapter 6   Numbers – Numere

The symbols for numbers in Romanian texts are the same as those used in English, with the exception of using the comma as the decimal separator and the period or the space (ideally a narrow space) for grouping digits by three in large numbers.

1. *Cardinal numbers*

The number 0 is called zero. Like in English, it requires the plural form of nouns: zero grade (zero degrees), with „grade" being the plural form of „grad".

Numbers 1 to 10

1	unu
2	doi
3	trei
4	patru
5	cinci
6	șase
7	șapte
8	opt
9	nouă
10	zece

When counting, the number names for 1 and 2 have the forms given ; however, when used in a sentence, they change according to the gender of the noun they modify or replace. It is worth noting that the two adjectival forms of the cardinal number for 1 (un and o) are identical with the corresponding indefinite articles.

un băiat- one boy, a boy

unul dintre băieți - one of the boys

o fată - one girl, a girl

una dintre fete - one of the girls

doi băieți - two boys

două fete - two girls

Numbers from 11 to 19

Unlike all other Romance languages, Romanian has a consistent way of naming the numbers from 11 to 19. These are obtained by joining three elements: the units, the word spre (meaning "towards" in Romanian), and the word for "ten".

For example, thirteen meaning treisprezece is trei + spre + zece, which literally means "three towards ten".

In day to day speech numbers are often used in informal speech, where the element '-sprezece is replaced by -șpe.

Number	*Formal Romanian*	*Informal Romanian*
11	unsprezece	unșpe
12	doisprezece	doișpe
13	treisprezece	treișpe
14	paisprezece	paișpe
15	cincisprezece	cinșpe (not cincișpe)
16	șaisprezece	șaișpe
17	șaptesprezece	șapteșpe, șaptișpe
18	optsprezece	optișpe, optâșpe
19	nouăsprezece	nouășpe

The number name for 12 given in the table is the masculine form; this is the only number in this range that also has a feminine form: douăsprezece (informal douășpe). However, the masculine form is sometimes used even with feminine nouns, especially when the number follows the noun it determines, as in ora doisprezece „12 o'clock" or clasa a doisprezecea („12th grade", see below for ordinal numbers); such use is considered incorrect.

Number names for 14 and 16 do not exactly follow the forming rule, possibly under the influence of the number names for 12 and 13. The forms patrusprezece and șasesprezece do exist, but are perceived as hypercorrect and very rarely used (one might hear them in telephone conversations, for the sake of correct transmission).

Numbers from 20 to 99

The numbers in this range that are multiple of 10 (that is, 20, 30, ..., 90) are named by joining the number of tens with the word zeci (the plural of zece) in a single word.

20	douăzeci
30	treizeci
40	patruzeci
50	cincizeci
60	șaizeci
70	șaptezeci
80	optzeci
90	nouăzeci

Notes

1. Cincizeci is often pronounced (but not written) cinzeci. Similarly, optzeci is often pronounced obzeci.

2. șaizeci does not follow the formation rule exactly. The expected form șasezeci does not exist.

3. This is a direct descendent of Latin vīgintī, which did not survive in Daco-Romanian.

The other numbers between 20 and 99 are named by combining three words: the number of tens, the conjunction și „and", and the units. For example, 42 is patruzeci și doi.

For those numbers whose unit figure is 1 or 2 the corresponding number name has two gender-dependent forms:

- masculine: treizeci și unu de bărbați „31 men";
  treizeci și doi de bărbați „32 men";
- feminine: treizeci și una de femei „31 women";
  treizeci și două de femei „32 women";
- neuter: treizeci și unu de grade „31 degrees";
  treizeci și două de grade „32 degrees".

Numbers from 100 to 999

Any given number from 100 to 999 can be named by first saying the hundreds and then, without any connecting word, the two-digit number of tens and units; for example

173 o sută șaptezeci și trei

365 trei sute șaizeci și cinci

248 două sute patruzeci și opt

Note that the word for „hundred" is sută, and that if the number of hundreds is 2 or larger, the plural sute is required. The noun sută itself is feminine and as such the numbers 100 and 200 are o sută and două sute.

Large numbers

The table below lists the numbers representing powers of 10 larger than 100, that have a corresponding single-word name. The word for 1000 is feminine, all the others are neuter; this is important in the number naming. In Romanian, neuter nouns behave like masculine in the singular and like feminine in the plural.

Number	*Singular*	*Plural*
100	o sută	(două) sute
1.000	o mie	(două) mii
1.000.000	un milion	(două) milioane

To say any cardinal number larger than 1000 the number is split in groups of three digits, from right to left (into units, thousands, millions, etc.), then the groups are read from left to right as in the example below.

12,345,678 (written in Romanian 12.345.678) = douăsprezece milioane trei sute patruzeci și cinci de mii șase sute șaptezeci și opt

When a digit is zero, the corresponding quantity is simply not pronounced:

101,010 (written in Romanian 101.010) = o sută una mii zece

In writing, the groups of three digits are separated by dots. The comma is used as decimal separator. This may be confusing for native English speakers, who use the two symbols the other way around.

Decimal fractions

Numbers represented as decimal fractions (for example 1.62) are expressed by reading in order the integer part, the decimal separator, and the fractional part. This is the same as in English, with the following exceptions:

The decimal separator is the comma, in Romanian virgulă. For example, 2.5 is written 2,5 and pronounced doi virgulă(comma) cinci.

The fractional part is read as a multi-digit number, not by saying each digit independently. For example, 3.14 (written 3,14) is pronounced trei virgulă paisprezece (literally three comma fourteen). However, when the number of decimals is too large, they can be read one by one as a string of digits: trei virgulă unu patru unu cinci nouă (3.14159).

Decimal fractions whose integer part is 0 (such as 0.6) are always written and pronounced in Romanian together with the initial zero: 0,6 is read zero virgulă şase, unlike English point six.

In some situations it is customary to say cu „with" instead of virgulă. For example, medical staff might be heard stating the body temperature in words like treizeci şi şapte cu cinci, meaning 37.5 °C.

2. *Percents*

Percentages (%) and permillages (‰) are read using the words la sută and la mie, like in the examples: cinci la sută (5%), nouă la mie (9‰). For percentages an alternative reading uses the neuter noun "procent", meaning 1%; the previous example becomes cinci procente.

Negative numbers

Negative numbers are named just like in English, by placing the word minus, pronounced minus, at the beginning: −10 m is minus zece metri.

Preposition „de"

Syntactically, when a cardinal number determines a noun and when the number has certain values, the preposition de (roughly equivalent to of) is inserted between the number name and the modified noun in a way similar to English hundreds of birds. Example: şaizeci de minute „sixty minutes".

The rules governing the use of preposition „de" are as follows:

For numbers from 0 to 19 „de" is not used. The same applies to numbers whose last two digits make a number in the range from 1 to 19. Examples: șapte case „seven houses", șaisprezece ani „16 years (old)", o sută zece metri „110 meters".

An exception to this rule is when the objects that are counted are symbols (letters, numbers). In this case, for better understanding the meaning, de can be used, although the practice is sometimes criticized. Example: se scrie cu doi de i „it's written with two i's", doi de zece „two tens", „two A grades".

Another exception is for numbers whose last two digits are 01, in which case an optional de is sometimes used. Examples: o mie una de ori „1001 times", o sută unu de dalmațieni „101 Dalmatians". In the latter case the choice might be influenced by euphony (avoidance of the alliteration).

For integer numbers from 20 to 100, preposition de is placed between the number name and the modified noun. The same applies to numbers whose last two digits are either 00 or make a number in the range from 20 to 99. Examples: douăzeci de metri „twenty meters", o mie de ori „a thousand times".

In technical contexts, to save space, the preposition de may be dropped, especially in writing: 200 metri plat „200 meters sprint". In expressing quantities using measurement unit symbols the preposition de is never written, but usually pronounced: 24 V $\rightarrow$ douăzeci și patru de volți „24 V, twenty-four volts".

For non-integer decimal numbers de is never used: 20,5 kg (read douăzeci virgulă cinci kilograme, „20.5 kg").

For negative numbers all the rules and exceptions above apply unchanged: −20 °C is minus douăzeci de grade Celsius, −5 m is minus cinci metri, −23,4 V is minus douăzeci și trei virgulă patru volți, etc.

The preposition de is also used within the syntax of the number itself, for stating the number of thousands, millions, billions, etc.: douăzeci de mii „twenty thousand" (also note the plural mii, unlike the singular thousand in English). The rules for this de are the same as those described above: it is used when the last two digits of the number of thousands, millions, etc. are 00 or 20–99. Again, in technical contexts, this de may be dropped: treizeci milioane euro „thirty million euros".

3. *Ordinal numbers*

The ordinal number (linguistics) is used to express the position of an object in an ordered sequence, as shown in English by words such as first, second, third, etc. In Romanian, with the exception of number 1, all ordinal numbers are named based on the corresponding cardinal number. Two gender-dependent forms exist for each number. The masculine form (also used with neuter nouns) ends in -lea, whereas the feminine form ends in -a. Starting from 2 they are preceded by the possessive article al / a.

Examples:

Am terminat de scris al treilea roman. „I finished writing the third novel."

Locuim la a cincea casă pe dreapta. „We live in the fifth house on the right."

Basic forms

The basic forms of the ordinal number are given in the table below. All other forms are made using them.

Number	Ordinal number	
	masculine	*feminine*
1st	primul	prima
2 nd	al doilea	a doua
3rd	al treilea	a treia
4th	al patrulea	a patra
5th	al cincilea	a cincea
6 th	al şaselea	a şasea
7th	al şaptelea	a şaptea
8th	al optulea	a opta
9th	al nouălea	a noua
10th	al zecelea	a zecea
100th	al o sutălea	a o suta
1000th	al o mielea	a o mia

Ordinal numbers in this range can be formed by modifying the corresponding cardinal number: the ending -zece is transformed into -zecelea and -zecea for the masculine and feminine ordinal number. Examples:

al unsprezecelea, a unsprezecea „the 11th";

al doisprezecelea, a douăsprezecea „the 12th", note the gender difference doi-, două-;

al treisprezecelea, a treisprezecea „the 13th", and so on.

Ordinal numbers in this range that have the unit digit 0 are formed by replacing the ending -zeci of the corresponding cardinal number with -zecilea and -zecea (masculine and feminine):

al douăzecilea, a douăzecea „the 20th";

al treizecilea, a treizecea „the 30th", and so on.

When the unit digit is not 0, the cardinal number is used for the tens and the ordinal number for the units. The only exception is when the unit digit is 1; in this case, instead of primul, prima a different word is used: unulea, una. Examples:

al douăzeci și unulea, a douăzeci și una „the 21st";

al douăzeci și doilea, a douăzeci și doua „the 22nd";

al douăzeci și treilea, a douăzeci și treia „the 23rd", and so on.

All other numbers

The general rule for ordinal number formation is to combine the following elements:

the possessive article al, a;

the cardinal number without the last pronounced digit;

the ordinal number corresponding to the last pronounced digit.

Examples:

101st: al o sută unulea, a o sută una;

210th: al două sute zecelea, a două sute zecea;

700th: al șapte sutelea, a șapte suta;

As seen in the last example above, the ordinal form of the plural of 100, 1000, etc. is needed for this process. These forms are:

Number	Ordinal number	
	masculine	*feminine*
n × 100	sutelea	suta
n × 1000	miilea	mia

Examples with large numbers:

1500th: al o mie cinci sutelea, a o mie cinci suta;

2000th: al două miilea, a două mia;

Reverse order

In certain situations the word order in expressing the ordinal number is reversed. This occurs when the object is not necessarily perceived as an element in a sequence but rather as an indexed object. For example, instead of al treilea secol the expression secolul al treilea „third century" is used. Note that the noun must have the definite article appended. Other examples:

etajul al cincilea „fifth floor";

partea a doua „second part, part two";

volumul al treilea „third volume, volume three";

grupa a patra „fourth group".

For simplification, often the cardinal number replaces the ordinal number, although some grammarians criticize this practice: The form secolul douăzeci is seen as an incorrect variant of secolul al douăzecilea „20th century".

For number 1, the form of the ordinal number in this reverse-order construction is întâi (or întîi), in both genders: deceniul întâi „first decade", clasa întâi „first grade". For the feminine, sometimes întâia is used, which until recently used to be considered incorrect by normative works.

The same reverse order is used when naming historical figures:

Carol I (read Carol Întâi);

Carol al II-lea (read Carol al Doilea).

As seen above, ordinal numbers are often written using Roman numerals, especially in this reverse order case. The ending specific to the ordinal numbers (-lea, -a) must be preserved and connected to the Roman numeral with a hyphen. Examples:

secolul al XIX-lea „19th century";

clasa a V-a „5th grade";

volumul I, volumul al II-lea „volume I, II".

Practice 5

I. Spell the numbers

1. 15 – ____________________________________

2. 46 – ____________________________________

3. 27 – ____________________________________

4. 39 – ____________________________________

5. 164 – ____________________________________

6. 572 – ____________________________________

7. 51 – ____________________________________

8. 102 – ____________________________________

9. 1206 – ____________________________________

10. 2019 – ____________________________________

II. Translate the sentences in English

1. Eu am şaptesprezece ani.

2. Acasă am trei câini şi două pisici.

3. M-am născut în anul o mie nouă sute optzeci şi doi.

4. Am plecat pentru douăzeci şi cinci de zile.

5. Acest restaurant este pe locul al doisprezecelea în lume.

6. Nu am citit volumul al II-lea încă.

7. Copilul meu are optsprezece ani şi este clasa a XII-a.

8. I-am explicat de o sută de ori deja.

9. Am citit „O mie şi una de nopţi".

10. Data de azi este douăzeci şi cinci luna a patra, două mii nouăsprezece.

III. Translate the sentences in Romanian.

1. The building was renovated in the 15th century.

2. I was born on May twenty second of nineteen thirty seven.

3. I am thirty years old and my son is seven years old.

4. I think I listened to it a thousend times.

5. You multiply by a milion here.

6. In 10th grade I changed schools.

7. I stay for fifty three days.

8. I stay on third floor in number one hundred five.

9. This dress is two hundred ninety three lei.

10. The dollar went down by 0.5 lei this week.

Chapter vocabulary

a citi – to read

a crede – to believe/ think

a sta –to stay

acasă – at home

an – year

building – clădire

clasă – grade / class / schoolroom

copil – child

dată – date

dolar – dollar

etaj – floor

loc – place

lume –world

multiplicare – multiplication

născut – born

noapte –night

renovată – renovated

secol – century

volum – volume

Chapter 7   Time and location – *Timp și locații*

1.   Locations – *Locații*

When we talk about nationalities, there are always different forms in the masculine and in the feminine form, so it's very important if we talk about a men or about a woman.

All the languages are feminine words, with the ending -ă.

Țara /Country	Naționalitatea / Natonality	Limba/ language spoken
România/ Romania	român / româncă	română
Statele Unite ale Americii/ United States of America	american / americancă	engleza
Marea Britanie (Anglia) / Great Britain (England)	englez / englezoaică	engleza
Franța / France	francez / franțuzoaică	franceza
Grecia / Greece	grec / grecoaică	greacă
Rusia / Russia	rus / rusoaică	rusă
Portugalia / Portugal	portughez / portugheză	portugheză
Polonia / Poland	polonez / poloneză	poloneză
Japonia / Japan	japonez / japoneză	japoneză
Italia / Italy	italian / italiancă	italiană
Germania / Germany	neamț / nemțoaică	germană
China / China	chinez / chinezoaică	chineză
Spania / Spain	spaniol / spanioloaică	spaniolă
Norvegia /Norway	novegian / norvegiancă	norvegiană
Turcia/ Turkey	turc/ turcoaică	turcă
Ungaria / Hungary	ungur/unguroaică	maghiară

Popular cities – Orașe populare

Antalya - Antalya

Bali – Bali

Bangkok - Bangkok

Barcelona - Barcelona

Bucharest – București

Budapest - Budapesta

Dubai - Dubai

Florence – Florența

Frankfurt – Frankfurt

Hong Kong – Hong Kong

Istanbul - Istambul

Lisbon –Lisabona

London - Londra

Milan - Milano

Moscow – Moscova

Munich – Munchen

New York – New York

Osaka - Osaka

Paris - Paris

Rome – Roma

Seoul – Seul

Singapore - Singapore

Tokyo – Tokyo

Venice – Veneția

Vienna – Viena

Warsaw – Varșovia

Land marks – Atracții turistice

Around the world

Arc de Triomphe –
Arcul de triumf

Berlin Wall –
Zidul Berlinului

Buckingham Palace –
Palatul Buckingham

Central Park – Parcul Central

Colosseum - Colosseum

Edinburgh Castle –
Castelul Edinburg

Eiffel Tower – Turnul Eiffel

Florence Cathedral –
Catedrala din Florența

Golden Gate Bridge –
Podul Golden Gate

Great Wall of China –
Marele zid Chinezesc

Leaning Tower of Pisa –
Turnul din Pisa

Louvre Museum – Muzeul Louvre

Mount Everest – Muntele Everest

Mount Fuj- Muntele Fuji

Mount Rushmore –
Muntele Reushmore

Niagara Falls – Cascada Niagara

Notre Dame –
Notre Dame

Pompeii -
Pompei

Pyramids of Giza –
Piramidele din Giza

The Great Sphinx –
Marele Sfinx

St. Peter's Basilica –
Bazilica Sf. Petru

The White House –
Casa Albă

Statue of Liberty –
Statuia Libertății

Trevi Fountain –
fântâna Trevi

Sydney Opera House –
Opera din Sydney

Vesuvius -
Vezuviu

The Forbidden City, China –
Orașul interzis, China

Windsor Castle –
Castelul Windsor

The Grand Canyon –
Marele Canion

In Romania

While there are many places worth viziting in Romania, here are some of the more popular ones.

Cetatea Alba Iulia –
Alba Iulia Fortress

Sarmizegetusa Regia –
Sarmizegetusa Regia

Castelul Peleș - Peleș Castle

Cetatea Făgăraș - Făgăraș Fortress

Castelul Bran – Bran Castle

Cetatea Râșnov – Râșnov Fortress

Castelul Corvinilor –
The Corvin Castle

Castrul Roman Arutela –
The Roman Castro Arutel

Delta Dunării – The Danube Delta

Palatul Culturii – Iași –
The Culture Palace, Iași

Mănăstirea Voroneț -
Voroneț Monastery

Arcul de Triumf București –
Arch of Triumph Bucharest

Salina Turda – Turda Salt Mine

Lacul Sf. Ana – St. Anne Lake

Muzeul Satului – București –
Village Museum Bucharest

Cascada Bigar – Bigar Waterfall

Castelul Cantacuzino - Bușteni –
Cantacuzino Castle, Bușteni

2. *Telling the time*

– Cât e ceasul / cât este ceasul? (What time is it?)
– Cât e ora / cât este ora? (What time is it?)
– Ce oră e / ce oră este? (What time is it?)
– Vă rog să îmi spuneți cât este ceasul? (Please tell me what time is it)
– Spuneți-mi vă rog, cât e ora? (Tell me please, what time is it?)
– Știți cât este ceasul? (Do you know what time is it?)
– Te rog să îmi spui cât este ceasul. (Please tell me what time is it)
– Spune-mi te rog, cât e ora? (Tell me please, what time is it?)
– Știi cât este ceasul? (Do you know what time is it?)

English	*Română*
It's one o'clock	Este ora unu
It's quarter past one	Este (ora) unu și un sfert
It's half past one	Este (ora) unu și jumătate
It's quarter to two	Este două fără un sfert
It's two o'clock	Este ora două
It's quarter past two	Este două și un sfert
It's half past two	Este două și jumătate
It's quarter to three	Este trei fără un sfert
It's three o'clock	Este ora trei
It's quarter past three	Este trei și un sfert
It's half past three	Este trei și jumătate
It's quarter to four	Este patru fără un sfert
It's four o'clock	Este ora patru
It's quarter past four	Este patru și un sfert
It's half past four	Este patru și jumătate
It's quarter to five	Este cinci fără un sfert
It's midnight	Este miezul nopții
in the morning	dimineața
in the afternoon	după-amiaza
in the evening	seara

Practice 6

I. Translate the sentences in English

1. De unde eşti?

2. Eu sunt din Statele Unite, din New York.

3. La ce oră ne întâlnim la gară?

4. La ora două vine trenul pentru Sibiu.

5. La ora trei şi un sfert ne întâlnim la castelul Peleş.

6. Eu nu sunt român dar încerc să învăţ română.

7. Ai vizitat Cetatea Râşnov?

8. Salina Turda este foarte mare.

9. În trei zile ne întâlnim pentru a vizita oraşul Bucureşti, în special Arcul de Triumf/

10. La miezul nopţii luminile se aprind în centrul istoric.

II. Translate the sentences in Romanian.

1. The Arch of Triumph in Bucharest is similar to the The Arch of Triumph in Paris.

2. The Bran Castle is also known as Dracula's Castle.

3. The Danube river starts from Germany and it flows the Black Sea.

4. At three o'clock we meet to visit The Culture Palace.

5. Between midnight and five o'clock in the morning the metro is closed.

6. The bus comes every half an hour.

7. Can you wake me up at quarter past ten please?

8. Please tell me what time it is.

9. Can you set the alarm clock to ring at quarter past seven?

10. Spanish, italian, french, partuguese and romanian are all latin based languages.

Chapter vocabulary

a curge -to flow

a încerca – to try

a seta – to set

arc –arch /bow

autobuz – bus

cascadă – waterfall

castel – castle

catedrală – cathredal

ceas – clock

cetate –fortress

între – between

jumătate – half

metrou – metrou

munte – mountain

muzeu – museum

oraş - city

oră – hour

piramidă – pyramid

râu – river

sat- village

sfert – quarter

similar – similar

statuie – statue

turn – tower

zid – wall

Chapter 8   *Weather - Vremea*

The climate is temperate continental in transition with oceanic climate, influenced by Scandinavian-Baltic weather, mediterranean climate and Black Sea weather. Thus, in the south mediterranean climate is felt, characterized by mild winters and stronger rainfalls (especially in autumn). In the south-east, the Black Sea climate occurs with rare heavy strong rains. In eastern regions, its continental character is less pronounced. In the north of the country (Maramureş and Bukovina), the effect of the Scandinavian-Baltic is felt, effecting a wetter and colder climate with cold winters. In the west of the country is manifested a more pronounced influence of low pressure systems generated over the Atlantic, causing moderate temperatures and stronger precipitation. Climate nuances are demonstrated on the steps of the altitude, the mountain ranges of the Carpathian arc being a cool mountain climate with high humidity throughout the year.

In Romania the temperature is measured in Celsius degrees. For example:

Afară sunt 30°C la soare.
Outside are 30°C in the sun.

Sunt 25 de grade celsius la umbră.
There are 25 degrees in the shade.

Starea vremii - Weather forecast (literaly weather state)

Nu plouă azi.
It doesn't rain today.

Afară e înnorat.
Outside is cloudy.

Bate vântul.
The wind is blowing.

In this case the word bate (beating) is used instead of suflă (blowing)

Se pot auzi tunete.
You can hear thunders.

De mâine vine ploaia.
Starting tomorrow the rain comes.

În această iarnă zăpada a bătut recordul.
This winter the snow broke the record.

Afară ninge de ieri. (ninge – snowing, zăpadă- snow)
Outside is snowing since yesterday.

Practice 7

I. **Translate the sentences in English**

1. Starea vremii spune că mâine va ploua.

2. Iarna aceasta a nins foarte mult.

3. Ai grijă să nu aluneci pe gheață.

4. A fost anunțat cod portocaliu de ninsoare și vânt.

5. Din cauza ploii vor fi inundații.

6. Începând cu săptămâna viitoare temperaturile
    vor fi peste 20 de grade celsius.

7. Prefer temperaturi scăzute.

8. Grindina a distrus culturile de porumb.

9. Cerul înnorat a acoperit orașul. Sper să nu plouă.

10. Aceasta este o dimineață însorită cu un cer senin.

II. Translate the sentences in Romanian.

1. The water temperature is going to reach
   23 degrees celsius this morning.

2. Water boils at 100 degrees Celsius

3. In minus 25 degrees Celsius is hard to keep yourself warm.

4. The wind is bringing in dark clouds.

5. After the storm the sky became clear.

6. This summer a draught was announced .

7. The excessive rains caused floods and mud slides in nearby
   villages.

8. A red code for frost and wind was announced earlier today.

9. The roads are foggy and dark.

10. The cool breeze feels good when the sun is so strong.

Chapter vocabulary

a distruge – to destroy

alunecări de teren – mud slides

anunţat – announced

breeze- briză

cald- warm

ceaţă – fog

cod –code

culturi – crops

drum – road

furtună – storm

gheaţă – ice

grindină – hail

inundaţie – flood

înnorat - cloudy

nor – cloud

ploaie –rain

polei – sleet

rece –cold

secetă –draught

senin – clear(sky)

soare - sun

stare –state

temperatură- temperature

tornadă – tornado

trăsnet – thunderbolt

tunet –thunder

umbră – shade

zăpadă – snow

Chapter 9   *Car trip – Excursie cu maşina*

1.   *Renting a car – Închirierea unei maşini*

Driving a rental car around Romania comes with a lot of advantages if you want to experience the country in a liberating yet comfortable way.

It's quite simple and hassle-free to rent a car in Romania. You'll need the following documents:

- valid identity card or passport – card de identitate sau paşaport
- valid driving license received at least one year ago – permis de conducere valabil , primit cu cel puţin un an în urmă

Keep in mind that the additional driver should present the same documents and also be present at the time of rental and pick up.

Road speed limits: 130 km/h on highways, 100 km/h on European and National roads, 90 km/h on Regional roads and 50 km/h inside localities.

You can aquire eighter an automatic transmission car or a manual. Rules and regulations are similar to those around the world. In Romania you drive on the right side of the road, it is mandatory to wear a safety belt(centură de siguranţă), both in the front and in the back and to use seats for children under 3 years old or under 135cm in height. Also, keep in mind that in Romania the blood alcohol limit is 0.0%.

Most car rentals have contracts in english but here are some useful phrases

Aş dori să închiriez o maşină cu transmisie automată.
I would like to rent a car with automatic transmission.

Ce preţ este pe zi?
What is the price per day?

Ce este acoperit de asigurare?
What does the insurance cover?

La ce oră trebuie să returnez maşina?
At what time do I have to return the car?

Maşina este echipată cu aer condiţionat şi CD player?
Is the car equiped with A/C and a CD player?

Aveşi o ofertă pentru un număr mai mare de zile?
Do you have a deal for a higher number of days?

Este inclus carburantul?
Is the fuel included?

Sunt taxat pe numărul de kilometri parcurşi?
Am I taxed on the mileage?

Se poate monta scaun pentru copii?
Can a child seat be installed?

Pe cine contactez în caz de urgenţă sau probleme cu maşina?
Who do I contact in case of emergency or problems with the car?

Această maşină are parbrizul ciobit.
This car has the windshield nicked.

Pot testa maşina înainte?
Can I test the car before?

Îmi poţi arăta interiorul?
Can you show me the inside?

Are roată de rezervă?
Does it have a spare tire?

2. *Buying petrol*

Most gas station are opened 24h and they accept both cash and card. In Romania you have to pump your own fuel.

Gasoline types

- Unleaded petrol (95/98 octane) -Benzină fără plumb
- Diesel – diesel
- GPL – GPL

Gas prices are usually listed by the liter, not gallon. There are also specific places that have only GPL

Scuzaţi-mă, unde este cea mai apropiată benzinărie?
Excuse me, where is the closest gas station?

Trebuie să fac plinul.
I need to fill it up.

Aş dori să plătesc pentru pompa numărul trei.
I would like to pay for pump number three.

Mă scuzaţi, am o problemă la pompa numărul cinci.
Escuse me, I have a problem at pump number five.

Am făcut pană, mă puteţi ajuta?
I got a flat tire, can you help me?

Practice 8

I. Translate the sentences in English

1. Bună ziua, aş dori să închiriez o maşină.
2. Vreau o maşină mică, de oraş.
3. Se poate monta un scaun pentru copii?
4. Cum se calculează preţul pe zi sau kilometraj?
5. Cu ce combustibil funcţionează, benzină?
6. Unde pot lăsa maşina la final?
7. Ce este acoperit de asigurare?
8. Pot testa maşina înainte de închiriere?
9. Aveţi în stoc maşină cu transmisie auotmată?
10. Unde este cea mai apropiată spălătorie?

II. Translate the sentences in Romanian.

1. Hello, do you have a van for rent?

2. How many seats does it have?

3. Does it use GPL?

4. I would like to pay for pump number six.

5. Do you have cleaning services?

6. Do you have windshield wiper fluid?

7. Where can I change the oil?

8. Where is the restroom?

9. Is the mileage unlimited in the contract?

10. What happens if the car is damaged?

III. Fill in the blanks

1. _______________ este crăpat.(windshield)

2. Întodeauna purtaţi _______________(the safety belt)

3. Trebuie să repoziţionez _______________
(rear view mirror)

4. Trebuie verificat _______________(the oil)

5. Cât de departe este _______________(gas station)

Chapter vocabulary

a închiria – to rent

a monta- to install

a poziţiona –to position

a purta – to wear

a repoziţiona – to reposition

a verifica- to check

apropiat – close (distance)

asigurare- insurance

automată – automatic

benizmă – petrol

benzinărie – gas station

centură – belt

contract – contract

dubă – van

kilometraj – mileage

manuală – manual

nelimitat –unlimited

oglindă- mirror

pană – flat tire

parbriz – windshield / windscreen

pompă – pump

portbagaj - trunk

rear view – retrovizoare

rezervă – spare

roată – tire

siguranţă – safety

spăşătorie – car wash

transmisie – transmission

ulei – oil

volan – steering wheel

Chapter 10 Medical emergencies – Urgențe medicale

1. *Human body – Corpul uman*

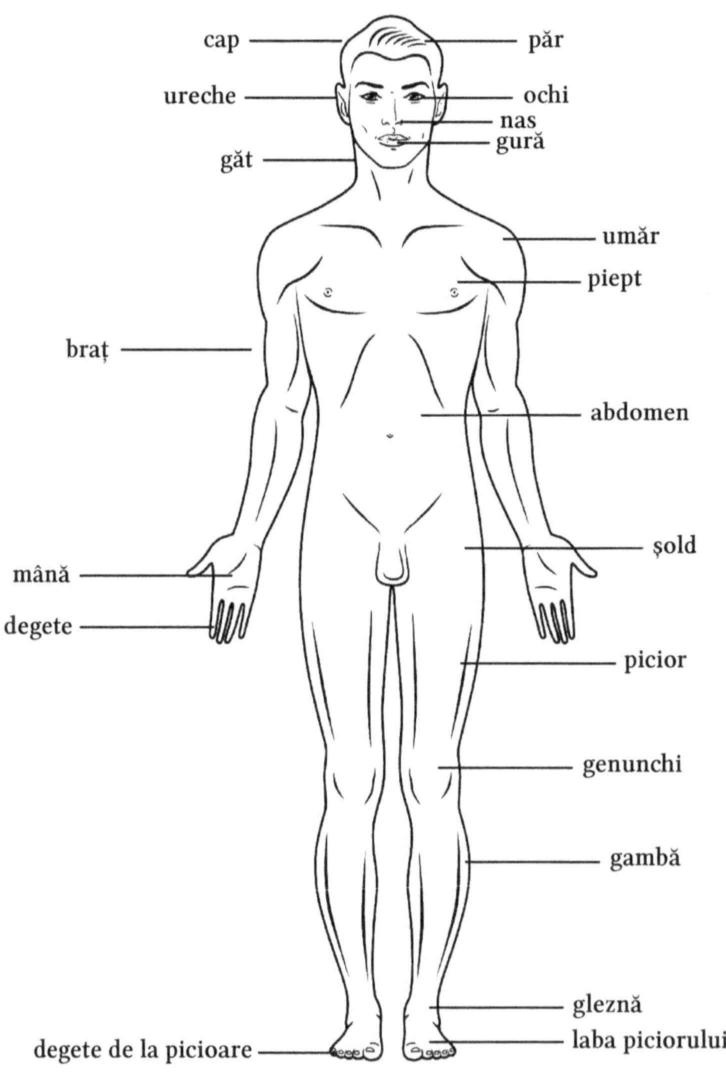

2. *Medical emergencies*

The emergency number in Romania is 112

For most ailments you can visit a farmacy and get help choosing the best medicine for the pain or superficial injury.

De trei zile am o mâncărime pe braţ.
Since three days ago I have an ich on my arm.

Am o iritaţie în zona burţii.
I have a rash in the belly area.

Am tuse seacă şi îmi curge nasul.
I have a dry cough and a runny nose.

Mă doare capul.
My head hurts.

Am probleme cu inima.
I have heart problems.

Sunt astmatic.
I am asthmatic.

M-am tăiat la deget.
I got cut on the finger.

Am nevoie de medicament pentru herpes.
I need cold sore medicine.

Am nevoie de medicament pentru răceală.
I need cold medicine.

Sunt alergic şi am nevoie de pastile.
I am alergic and I need pills.

Aş dori un medicament pentru dureri de cap fără aspirină.
I would like a headache medicine without aspirin please.

Mi-a intrat un cui în talpă.
I got a nail in my sole.

O cremă cu protecţie solară pentru corp vă rog.
A body cream with UV protection please.

Unde este cel mai apropiat spital?
Where is the closest hospital?

Aş dori să vorbesc cu un doctor despre problema mea.
I would like to speak with a doctor about my problem.

Am avut accident vascular cerebral în trecut.
I had a stroke in the past.

Preferaţi tablete sau sirop?
Would you preffer tablets or syrup?

Prietena mea şi-a pierdut cunoştinţa!
My friend is unconscious!

For an emergency call the number 112 and follow the instructions. It has an availbility for english.

If you have an illness or prescription pills it is good to make sure to have a written document mentioning it.

Practice 9

I. Translate the sentences in English

1. Sunt anemică, aveţi suplimente?
2. Am răcit şi am puţină febră.
3. Aveţi termometre?
4. Am nevoie de o cutie de ibuprofen şi un sirop de tuse.
5. Unde este cel mai apropiat spital sau cabinet medical?
6. Ce medicament îmi puteţi recomanda pentru dureri de stomac?
7. La cât timp se iau aceste pastile?
8. Care este doza recomandată?
9. Am nevoie de o programare la un medic stomatolog/dentist.
10. Pentru cât timp trebuie menţinut?

II. Translate the sentences in Romanian.

1. My husband is unconscious and we need an ambulance.

2. We were in a car accident and I can't open the door.

3. I can't feel my arm.

4. I think I broke my arm when I went skiing.

5. I need an anti inflammatory for my foot.

6. I feel a sharp pain in my kidney.

7. I burned my hand while cooking, is there any aloe vera lotion?

8. I have rheumatism in my left knee.

9. I need eye drops

10. I have a friend in the emergency room. Can you tell me the way?

Chapter vocabulary

abdomen – abdomen

accident – accident

ambulanță – ambulance

anemică –anemic

ascuțit – sharp

asistentă – nurse

barbă – chin

braț - arm

buze – lips

cabinet medical – doctor's office

cameră – room

cap – head

călcâi - heel

creier – brain

degete de la picioare – toes

degete -fingers

dinți –teeth

doctor –doctor

durere – pain

febră – fever

ficat – liver

gât – throat

gât –neck

geană – eyelash

genunchi – knee

gleznă – anckle

gură - mouth

herpes – herpes/cold sore

inimă – heart

iritație –rash

mână –hand

mâncărime – itch

nas -nose

obraz – cheeck

pastile -pills

păr – hair

picături – drops

picior – leg

picior (laba piciorului) –foot

piept – chest

plamân – lung

prescripție – prescription

programare –appointment

rinichi – kidney

shold –hip

sirop – syrup

sprânceană – eyebrow

stomac – stomach

stomatolog - dentist

suplimente – supliments

tablete – tablets

talpă – sole

umăr – shoulder

unghie –nail

ureche –ear

urgențe – emergencies

vascular – vascular

Glossary English – Romanian

abdomen – abdomen

access – acces

accident – accident

allergy – alergie

also – şi

also – tot

ambulance– ambulanţă

anckle– glezna

and – şi

anemic –anemică

announced – anunţat

another – alt

appointment –programare

april – aprilie

arch – arc

arm - braţ

at home – acasă

august – august

automatic – automată

available – disponibil

away – plecat

bag – geantă

bag – pungă

beaver – castor

beer – bere

before – înainte

belt – centură

between – între

book – carte

born – născut

bottle – sticlă

bow – arc

brain – creier

bread – pâine

breeze – briză

broken – spart

broth – ciorbă

brother – frate

building – clădire

bus – autobuz

cabbage rolls – sarmale

cake – prăjitură

car – maşină

car wash – spăşătorie

cash – numerar

castle – castel

cat – pisică

cathredal – catedrală

century – secol

chair – scaun

check – notă de plată

cheeck – obraz

cheek – obraz

cheese – brânză

cheese – caşcaval

chest - piept

chicken – găină

chicken – pui

child – copil

chin– barbă

city – oraș

class– clasă

clear(sky) – senin

clock – ceas

clogged – înfundată

close (distance) – apropiat

closed – închis

cloud – nor

cloudy – înnorat

coat – palton

code – cod

coffee – cafea

coke – cola

cold – rece

compared – comparativ

contract – contract

corner – colț

crops – culturi

cup – cană

dark colors – închis

date – dată

days – zile

december – decembrie

dentist - stomatolog

diabetus – diabet

doctor –doctor

doctor's office– cabinet medical

dog – câine

dollar – dolar

double – dublă

down – jos

draught – secetă

drink – băutură

drinks – băuturi

drops – picături

duck – rață

ear –ureche

egg – ou

emergencies – urgențe

englishman – englez

evening – seară

everything – tot

extra – suplimentară

eyebrow – sprânceană

eyelash – geană

fan – fan

farmerțs market – piață

father – tată

february – februarie

fever– febră

fingers- degete

fish – pește

flat tire – pană

flood – inundație

floor (for apartment floors only) – etaj

fog – ceață

food – mâncare

foot - picior (laba piciorului)

English	Romanian
fortress – cetate	house – casă
friday – vineri	human – om
fries – cartofi prăjiți	hunger – foame
fur – blană	ice – gheață
garlic – usturoi	ice cream – înghețată
gas station – benzinărie	included – inclus
gift – cadou	information – informație
girl – fată	insurance – asigurare
give a call – suna	intelligent – inteligent
gluten – gluten	intolerant – intoleranță
gmo – gmo	isolated – izolată
good – bună	itch- mâncărime
grade – clasă	jacket – sacou
hail – grindină	january – ianuarie
hair – păr	jasmine – iasomie
half – jumătate	juice – suc
hand –mână	july – iulie
head – cap	june – iunie
head–cap	ketchup – ketchup
heart– inimă	key – cheie
heel - călcâi	kidney– rinichi
here – aici	kilogram – kilogram
hero – erou	kilometre – kilometru
herpes/cold sore - herpes	kitchen – bucătărie
hip –shold	knee – genunchi
honey – miere	lactose – lactoză
hot – fierbinte	last week – săptămâna trecută
hot chocolate – ciocolată caldă	late – târziu
hotel – hotel	laundry room – spălătorie
hour – oră	left – plecat

left – stânga	mother – mamă
left over – rest	mountain – munte
leg – picior	mouth- gură
lemonade – limonadă	movie – film
less – puțin	much – mult
light colors – deschis	mud slides – alunecări de teren
lips– buze	mulled wine – vin fiert
litre – litru	multiplication – multiplicare
little – puțin	museum – muzeu
liver– ficat	mustard – muștar
lowered – plecat	nail - unghie
luggage – bagaj	nature – natură
lung– plamân	neck– gât
man – bărbat	need – nevoie
manual – manuală	next week – săptămâna viitoare
march – martie	night – noapte
may – mai	noise – zgomot
mayo – maioneză	nose - nas
menu – meniu	nose – nas
merchendise – marfã	notebook – caiet
metro – metrou	november – noiembrie
mile – milă	nurse - asistentă
mileage – kilometraj	oats – ovăz
milk – lapte	october – octombrie
mirror – oglindă	oil – ulei
monday – luni	olive oil – ulei de măsline
money – bani	onion – ceapă
month – lună	open – deschis
more – în plus	package – pachet
morning – dimineață	pain– durere

panel – panou

park – parc

password – parolă

pasta – paste

payment – plată

peanuts – alune

people – lume

pepper – piper

peppers(bell) – ardei

petrol – benizbă

piece – bucată

 pills- pastile

place – loc

plum brandy – țuică

pound (currency) - liră

pound (for weight) - livră

prescription - prescripție

priest – popă

problem – problemă

proud – mândru

pump – pompă

pyramid – piramidă

quarter – sfert

radio – radio

rain – ploaie

rash- iritație

rear view – retrovizoare

recomendation – recomandare

red – roșu

renovated – renovată

restaurant – restaurant

rice – orez

right – drapta

river – râu

road – drum

room – camera

room - cameră

safety – siguranță

salt – sare

saturday – sâmbătă

schoolroom – clasă

seeds – semințe

september – septembrie

sesame – susan

set – set

shade – umbră

shared – comună

sharp– ascuțit

sheet of paper – foaie

shoe – pantof

shoulder – umăr

shoulder – umăr

shrimp – creveți

similar – similar

sister – sora

size – mărime

skirt – fustă

sleet – polei

smart – deștept

smooth – fin

snow – zăpadă

soft drinks – băuturi carbogazoase

sole – talpă

something – ceva

something else – altceva

sorry – scuze

soup – supă

sour cream – smântână

soy – soia

spare – rezervă

sparkling water – apă minerală

spicy – iute

spicy – picant

star – stea

start – încep

state – stare

statue – statuie

steak – friptură

steering wheel – volan

stew – tocăniţă

still – încă

still – tot

still water – apă plată

stomach – stomac

store – magazin

storm – furtună

story – poveste

strawberries – căpşuni

student – studentă

sugar – zahăr

sun – soare

sunday – duminică

supermarket – supermarket

supliments– suplimente

sweetener – îndulcitor

syrup –sirop

table – masă

tablets– tablete

talks – vorbeşte

taste – gust

tea – ceai

teeth - dinţi

temperature – temperatură

there – acolo

this week – săptămâna aceasta

throat- gât

thunder – tunet

thunderbolt – trăsnet

thursday – joi

tire – roată

to add – în plus

to allow – a permite

to believe – a crede

to call – a suna

to check – a verifica

to choose – a alege

to compare – a compara

to destroy – a distruge

to find – a găsi

to flow – a curge

to grow – a creşte

to install – a monta

to position – a poziţiona

to read – a citi

to rent – a închiria

to reposition – a repoziţiona

to serve – a servi

to set – a seta

to smoke – a fuma

to stay – a sta

to think – a crede

to try a – încerca

to verify – a verifica

to wear – a purta

today – astăzi

toes - degete de la picioare

tomato – roşie

tomorrow – mâine

too – şi

tornado – tornadă

towel – prosop

tower – turn

transmission – transmisie

tree – copac

triple – triplă

true – adevărat

trunk – portbagaj

trust – încredere

truth – adevăr

tuesday – marţi

unlimited – nelimitat

up – sus

vacation – vacanţă

van – dubă

vascular – vascular

vegetarian – vegetarian

village – sat

vinegar – oţet

visit – vizită

volume – volum

wall – zid

warm – cald

waterfall – cascadă

wednesday – miercuri

week – săptămână

wheat – grâu

white – alb

windscreen – parbriz

windshield – parbriz

wine – vin

wine mixed with sparkling water – şpriţ

without – fără

work – treabă

world – lume

year – an

yesterday – ieri

Glossary Romanian -English

a alege – to choose

a citi – to read

a compara – to compare

a crede – to believe

a crede – to think

a crește – to grow

a curge – to flow

a distruge – to destroy

a fuma – to smoke

a găsi – to find

a încerca – to try

a închiria – to rent

a monta – to install

a permite – to allow

a poziționa – to position

a purta – to wear

a repoziționa – to reposition

a servi – to serve

a seta – to set

a sta – to stay

a suna – to call

a verifica – to check

a verifica – to verify

abdomen – abdomen

acasă – at home

acces – access

accident – accident

acolo – there

adevăr – truth

adevărat – true

aici – here

alb – white

alergie – allergy

alt –another

altceva – something alse

alune – peanuts

alunecări de teren – mud slides

ambulanță – ambulance

an – year

anemică –anemic

anunțat – announced

apă minerală – sparkling water

apă plată – still water

aprilie – april

apropiat – close (distance)

arc – arch

arc – bow

ardei – pepper(bell)

ascuțit – sharp

asigurare – insurance

asistentă – nurse

astăzi – today

august – august

autobuz – bus

automată – automatic

bagaj – luggage

bani – money

barbă – chin

bărbat – man

băutură – drink

băuturi – drinks

băuturi carbogazoase – soft drinks

benizbă – petrol

benzinărie – gas station

bere – beer

blană – fur

braț - arm

brânză – cheese

briză – breeze

bucată – piece

bucătărie – kitchen

bună – good

buze – lips

cabinet medical – doctor's office

cadou – gift

cafea – coffee

caiet – notebook

cald – warm

camera – room

cameră – room

cană – cup

cap – head

cap – head

carte – book

cartofi prăjiți - fries

casă – house

cascadă – waterfall

castel – castle

castor – beaver

cașcaval – cheese

catedrală – cathredal

călcâi - heel

căpșuni – strawberries

câine – dog

ceai – tea

ceapă – onion

ceas – clock

ceață – fog

centură – belt

cetate – fortress

ceva – something

cheie – key

ciocolată caldă – hot chocolate

ciorbă – broth

clasă – class

clasă – grade

clasă – schoolroom

clădire – building

cod – code

cola – coke

colț – corner

comparativ – compared

comună – shared

contract – contract

copac – tree

copil – child

creier – brain

creveți – shrimp

culturi – crops

dată – date

decembrie – december

degete de la picioare – toes

degete –fingers

deschis – light colors

deshis – open

deștept – smart

diabet – diabetus

dimineață – morning

dinți –teeth

disponibil – available

doctor –doctor

dolar – dollar

drapta – right

drum – road

dubă – van

dublă – double

duminică – sunday

durere – pain

englez – englishman

erou – hero

etaj – floor (for apartment floors only)

fan – fan

fată – girl

fără – without

febră – fever

februarie – february

ficat – liver

fierbinte – hot

film – movie

fin – smooth

foaie – sheet of paper

foame – hunger

frate – brother

friptură – steak

furtună – storm

fustă – skirt

găină – chicken

gât – throat

gât –neck

geană – eyelash

geantă – bag

genunchi – knee

gheață – ice

glezna – anckle

gluten – gluten

gmo – gmo

grâu – wheat

grindină – hail

gură - mouth

gust – taste

herpes – herpes/cold sore

hotel – hotel

ianuarie – january

iasomie – jasmine

ieri – yesterday

inclus – included

informație – information

inimă – heart

inteligent – intelligent

intoleranţă – intolerant

inundaţie – flood

iritaţie –rash

iulie – july

iunie – june

iute – spicy

izolată – isolated

în plus – more

în plus – to add

înainte – before

încă – still

încep – start

închis – closed

închis – dark colors

încredere – trust

îndulcitor – sweetener

înfundată – clogged

îngheţată – ice cream

înnorat – cloudy

între – between

joi – thursday

jos – down

jumătate – half

ketchup – ketchup

kilogram – kilogram

kilometraj – mileage

kilometru – kilometre

lactoză – lactose

lapte – milk

limonadă – lemonade

liră – pound (currency)

litru – litre

livră – pound (for weight)

loc – place

lume – people

lume – world

lună – month

luni – monday

magazin – store

mai – may

maioneză – mayo

mamă – mother

manuală – manual

marfă – merchendise

martie – march

marţi – tuesday

masă – table

maşină – car

mărime – size

mâine – tomorrow

mână –hand

mâncare – food

mâncărime – itch

mândru – proud

meniu – menu

metrou – metrou

miercuri – wednesday

miere – honey

milă – mile

mult – much

multiplicare – multiplication

munte – mountain

muștar – mustard

muzeu – museum

nas – nose

nas -nose

natură – nature

născut – born

nelimitat – unlimited

nevoie – need

noapte – night

noiembrie – november

nor – cloud

notă de plată – check

numerar – cash

obraz – cheeck

obraz – cheek

octombrie – october

oglindă – mirror

om – human

oraș – city

oră – hour

orez – rice

oțet – vinegar

ou – egg

ovăz – oats

pachet – package

palton - coat

pană – flat tire

panou – panel

pantof – shoe

parbriz – windscreen

parbriz – windshield

parc – park

parolă – password

paste – pasta

pastile -pills

păr – hair

pâine – bread

pește – fish

piață – farmerțs market

picant – spicy

picături – drops

picior – leg

picior (laba piciorului) –foot

piept – chest

piper – pepper

piramidă – pyramid

pisică – cat

plamân – lung

plată – payment

plecat – away

plecat – left

plecat – lowered

ploaie – rain

polei – sleet

pompă – pump

popă – priest

portbagaj – trunk

poveste – story

prăjitură – cake

prescripție – prescription

problemă – problem

programare –appointment

prosop – towel

pui – chicken

pungă – bag

puțin – less

puțin – little

radio – radio

rață – duck

râu – river

rece – cold

recomandare – recomendation

renovată – renovated

rest – left over

restaurant- restaurant

retrovizoare – rear view

rezervă – spare

rinichi – kidney

roată – tire

roșie – tomato

roșu – red

sacou – jacket

sare – salt

sarmale – cabbage rolls

sat – village

săptămâna aceasta - this week

săptămâna trecută - last week

săptămâna viitoare - next week

săptămână - week

sâmbătă - saturday

scaun – chair

scuze – sorry

seară – evening

secetă – draught

secol – century

semințe – seeds

senin – clear(sky)

septembrie – september

set – set

sfert – quarter

shold –hip

siguranță – safety

similar – similar

sirop – syrup

smântână – sour cream

soare – sun

soia – soy

sora – sister

spart – broken

spălătorie – laundry room

spășătorie – car wash

sprânceană – eyebrow

stare – state

statuie – statue

stânga – left

stea – star

sticlă – bottle

stomac – stomach

stomatolog - dentist

studentă – student

suc – juice

suna – give a call

supă – soup

supermarket – supermarket

suplimentară – extra

suplimente – supliments

sus – up

susan – sesame

şi – also

şi – and

şi – too

şpriţ - wine mixed with sparkling water

tablete – tablets

talpă – sole

tată – father

târziu – late

temperatură – temperature

tocăniţă – stew

tornadă – tornado

tot – also

tot – everything

tot – still

transmisie – transmission

trăsnet – thunderbolt

treabă – work

triplă – triple

tunet – thunder

turn – tower

ţuică – plum brandy

ulei – oil

ulei de măsline – olive oil

umăr – shoulder

umăr – shoulder

umbră – shade

unghie –nail

ureche –ear

urgenţe – emergencies

usturoi – garlic

vacanţă – vacation

vascular – vascular

vegetarian – vegetarian

vin – wine

vin fiert – mulled wine

vineri – friday

vizită – visit

volan – steering wheel

volum – volume

vorbeşte – talks

zahăr – sugar

zăpadă – snow

zgomot – noise

zid – wall

zile – days

Practice answer key

Practice 1

I. Choose the right word

1.	b)	6.	a)
2.	c)	7.	b)
3.	c)	8.	c)
4.	a)	9.	b)
5.	b)	10.	b)

II. Translate the following text.

1. Bună dimineața.
2. Eu sunt Andrei și el este Peter. Încântat de cunoștință/
3. Noi suntem din Anglia. E mai rece ca România. Îți place Anglia?
4. Excuse me. We visit România.
5. Can you tell us where the big park is? We want to see the lake.
6. I thank you.

III. Fill in the blanks.

1.	Mai frumoasă	6.	buni
2.	român	7.	mândri
3.	mai inteligent	8.	mei
4.	are	9.	Te
5.	au	10.	Pentru tine

Practice 2

I. Fill in the blanks.

1.	vreau	6.	fără maioneză
2.	este	7.	supă
3.	fără	8.	au lapte
4.	cu mai multe/ extra ciuperci	9.	picantă
5.	cartofi prăjiți.	10.	pâine

II. Translate the following to English

1. Good afternoon. I would like a glass of red wine and a coffee.
2. I do not want fries. I would like them baked.
3. I am allergic to egg, can it be replaced?
4. I would like a glass of plum brandy.
5. Do you have a vegetarian meniu?
6. A strawberry ice cream please.
7. Is the onion stew spicy?
8. Can you bring me a brown sugar packet?
9. Do you have sweetener or honey?
10. A potion of cabbage roll with sour cream.

III. Translate the following to Romanian

1. Bună, aş dori un ceai de iasomie.
2. Pot avea meniul de băuturi?
3. Aş dori o friptură în sânge.
4. Pot avea încă o limonadă?
5. Cât de mare este porţia?
6. Pot avea nota, te rog?
7. Serviţi creveţi?
8. Conţine gluten?
9. Poate avea altă furculiţă?
10. Aveţi un meniu pentru copii?

Practice 3

I. Fill in the blanks.

1. De o persoană
2. pătură
3. animal de companie
4. micul dejun
5. izolată fonic
6. este
7. Geamul
8. lună
9. Sâmbătă
10. Săptămâna trecută
11. disponibilă
12. prosop
13. rezervarea
14. cheia
15. cina

II. Translate the phrases into English.

1. Good evening, I would like to book a triple room for Wednesday. I saw that pets are allowed, is that true?

2. The available room, is it for non-smokers?

3. We have a problem and we will arrive later, can we have the check in then?

4. Can we have breakfast if we pay?

5. Do you have available room for next month?

6. Can I smoke in the room?

7. Is the kitchen shared?

8. Where is the shared bathroom?

9. The laundry room is always open?

10. Can you give me one more set of towels please?

III. Translate the phrases into Romanian.

1. Bună, pot rezerva o cameră dublă cu baie comună pentru marți, săptămâna asta?

2. Este posibil să avem check out-ul mai târziu?

3. Este camera de la etaj izolată fonic?

4. Apa caldă nu merge în cameră.

5. Se poate repara azi scurgerea înfundată?

6. Până când se servește micul dejun?

7. Am acces la bucătăria comună toată ziua?

8. Internetul nu funcționează în camera mea.

9. Baia are cadă sau duș?

10. Când este check out-ul?

Practice 4

I. Translate the following phrases in English

1. Give me a kilogram of potatoes and two of onions
2. Is this all you have?
3. How muchi s a litre of milk?
4. Can you put that piece?
5. I want 500 grams of olives.
6. Do you have change?
7. Where is the market?
8. Until the amount put apples.
9. Can I choose?
10. Are you the one growing the vegetables?

II. Translate the phrases in Romanian.

1. Cât este kilogramul de roșii?
2. Aș dori să cumpăr o pungă de fursecuri.
3. Aveți o mărime diferită?
4. Acceptați numerar?
5. Pot avea două din acelașii fel?
6. Un kilogram de cartofi și unul de ceapă vă rog.
7. Il aveți în sticle de 2 litri?
8. Două beri la 330 mililitri vă rog.
9. Cât ete cea de 330 de mililitri comparativ cu cea de 500 de mililitri?
10. Este o bucată mai ieftină decât pachetul?

Practice 5

I. Spell the numbers in romanian

1. Cincisprezece
2. Patruzeci și șase
3. Douăzeci și șapte
4. Treizeci și nouă
5. O sută șaizeci și patru
6. Cinci sute șaptezeci și doi
7. Cincizeci și unu
8. O sută doi
9. O mie două sute șase
10. Două mii nouăsprezece

II. Translate the sentences in English

1. I am 17 years old
2. At home I have three dogs and two cats
3. I was born in the year1982
4. I left for 25 days
5. This restaurant is on 12th place in the world.
6. I have not red the 2nd volume yet.
7. My child is 18 years old and is in 12th grade.
8. I already explained it a hundred times.
9. I red „One thousand and one nights" .
10. Today's date is 25, 4th month 2019

III. Translate the sentences in Romanian.

1. Clădirea a fost renovată îm secolul al XV-lea.
2. M-am născut în Mai douăzeci și cinci, o mie nouă sute treizeci și șapte
3. Eu am treizeci de ani iar fiul meu are șapte ani.
4. Cred că am ascultat-o de o mie de ori.
5. Multimplici cu un milion aici.
6. În clasa a X-a am schimbat școala.
7. Stau pentru cincizeci și trei de zile
8. Stau la etajul al treilea la numărul o sută cinci.
9. Această rochie este două sute nouăzeci și trei lei.
10. Dolarul a scăzut cu 0 virgulă cinci lei săptămâna asta

Practice 6

I. Translate the sentences in English

1. Where are you from?

2. I am from the United States, from New York.

3. At what time do we meet at the train station?

4. At two o'clock arrives the train for Sibiu.

5. At quarte past three we meet at the Peleş Castle.

6. I am not romanian but I try to learn Romanian.

7. Have you visited Râşnov Fortress?

8. Turda Salt mine is very big.

9. In three days we meet to visit Bucharest city, especially the Arch of Triumph.

10. At midnight the lights turn on in the historic centre.

II. Translate the sentences in Romanian.

1. Arcul de Triumf în Bucureşti este similar cu Arcul de Triumf în Paris.

2. Castelul Bran este cunoscut şi sub denumirea de Castelul lui Dracula.

3. Râul Dunăre începe din Germania şi curge în Marea Neagră.

4. La ora trei ne întâlnim pentru a vizita Palatul Culturii.

5. Între miezul nopţii şi ora cinci dimineaţa metroul este închis.

6. Autobuzul vine la fiecare jumătate de oră.

7. Poţi să mă trezeşti la zece şi un sfert te rog?

8. Spune-mi cât este ceasul te rog.

9. Poţi seta alarma să sune la şapte şi un sfert?

10. Spaniola, italiana, franceza, portugheza şi româna sunt toate limbi latine.

Practice 7

I. Translate the sentences in English

1. The weather forecast says that tomorrow will rain
2. This winter it snowed a lot.
3. Be careful not to slip on the ice.
4. Orange code was announced for snow and wind.
5. Because of the rain there will be floods.
6. Starting with next week the temperatures
    will be over 20 degrees celsius
7. I preffer lower temperatures.
8. The hail destroyed the corn crops.
9. The cloudy sky covered the city, I hope it will not rain.
10. This is a sunny morning with a clear sky.

II. Translate the sentences in Romanian

1. Temperatura apei va atinge 23 de grade celsius dimineața asta.
2. Apa fierbe la 100 de grade celsius.
3. La minus 25 de grade celsius este greu să te menții cald.
4. Vântul aduce nori întunecați.
5. După furtună cerul a devenit senin.
6. Vara asta a fost anunțată o secetă.
7. Ploile excesive au cauzat inundații și alunecări
    de teren în sate apropiate.
8. Cod roșu pentru gheață și vânt a fost anunțat mai devreme azi.
9. Drumurile sunt încețoșate și întunecate.
10. Briza răcoroasă de simte bine când soarele este așa puternic.

Practice 8

I. Translate the sentences in English

1. Good day, I would like to rent a car.
2. I would like a small, city car.
3. Can a child seat be installed?
4. How is the price done, per day or mileage?
5. With what fuel does it function, petrol?
6. Where can I leave the car at the end?
7. What is covered by the insurance?
8. Can I test the car before renting it?
9. Do you have in stock a car with automatic transmision?
10. Where is the closest car wash?

II. Translate the sentences in Romanian

1. Bună, aveți dubă de închiriat?
2. Câte locuri are?
3. Folosește GPL?(red as „ge pe le")
4. Aş dori să plătesc pentru pompa numărul şase.
5. Aveți servicii de curăţare?
6. Aveți lichid pentru parbriz?
7. Unde pot schimba uleiul?
8. Unde este toaleta?
9. Kilometrajul este nelimitat în contract?
10. Ce se întâmplă dacă maşina este avariată?

III. Fill in the blanks

1. parbriz
2. centură de siguranţă
3. oglinda retrovizoare
4. uleiul
5. benzinăria

Practice 9

I. Translate the sentences in English

1. I am anemic, do you have supplements?
2. I have a cold and a slight fever.
3. Do you have thermometres?
4. I need a box of ibuprofen and a cough syrup.
5. Where is the slosest hospital or docotor's office?
6. What medicine can you recommend me for stomach ache?
7. In what interval do I take this pills?
8. Which is the recommended dose?
9. I need an apointment for a dentist.
10. For how long does it have to be maintained?

II. Translate the sentences in Romanian.

1. Soțul meu și-a pierdut cunoștința și avem nevoie de o ambulanță.
2. Am fost într-un accident de mașină și nu pot deschide ușa.
3. Nu îmi simt mâna.
4. Cred că mi-am rupt mâna când am fost la schi.
5. Am nevoie de un anti inflamator pentru piciorul meu.
6. Simt o durere ascuțită în rinishi.
7. M-am ars la mână cțnd găteam, este vre-o loțiune cu aloe vera?
8. Am reumatism la genunchiul stâng.
9. Am nevoie de picături pentru ochi.
10. Am un/o prieten/ă în camera de urgențe.
    Îmi puteți spune direcția?

Bibliography

1. Ramona Gönczöl-Davies and Dennis Deletant

2. Colloquial Romanian:The Complete Course for beginners Basic

3. Romanian Language Lessons / Peace Corps Moldova

4. Augerot, J. E. 2000. Romanian / Limba Română. A Course in Modern Romanian. Iaşi, Oxford, Portland: The Center for Romanian Studies.

5. Bălănescu, O. 1998. Limba română pentru străini. Bucureşti: Fiat Lux.

6. Dorobăţ, A., Fotea, M. 1999. Limba română de bază. Manual pentru studenţii străini. Iaşi: Institutul European.

7. Dana Cojocaru Romanian Grammar / Slavic and East European Language Research Center (SEELRC), Duke University, 2003

www.ingramcontent.com/pod-product-compliance
Lightning Source LLC
Chambersburg PA
CBHW071212130726
47998CB00002B/719